Socialist History Society

The Labour Party in Historical Perspective

Edited by *David Morgan*

Contributors
> *John Belchem*
> *Duncan Bowie*
> *Keith Laybourn*
> *Dave Lyddon*
> *David Morgan*
> *Graham Taylor*
> *Willie Thompson*

Socialist History
Occasional Publication 42

SOCIALIST
HISTORY
SOCIETY

Published by
The Socialist History Society

ISBN 978-0-9930104-7-7

May 2018

Contents

Preface

It is now over one hundred years since the Labour Party adopted its Constitution drawn up by Sidney Webb with its contentious Clause IV, part 4, committing the party to the common ownership of the means of production, distribution and exchange, although to be achieved at some undefined future.

Over the decades the party's march to the New Jerusalem has taken a distinctly circuitous route. In recent years, Labour has radically shifted gear from espousing a form of neo-liberalism and the search for free market solutions to domestic policy challenges under New Labour to a return to more traditional socialist aims and values under the leadership of Jeremy Corbyn and John McDonnell. An unprecedented upsurge in membership has transformed the party into a mass political organisation at least in numerical terms.

The idea for this publication emerged following discussions within the SHS about the need for the Labour Party and its new generation of activists to learn from their own history. In these pages the contributors, all broadly sympathetic to the party but with no common position, address aspects of Labour's record in government and its political campaigning for social change, focusing on its achievements while not neglecting its weaknesses.

In terms of domestic reforms there have been many notable successes for which the party can claim credit: the welfare state, the NHS, civil rights legislation, equal pay for women, comprehensive education, the Open University and the Arts Council. With regards to foreign policy, the party's achievements have been more mixed at least from a socialist point of view: strong defence, the atomic bomb, American bases on British soil, NATO membership, the special relationship will the United States and regime change in Iraq.

Labour has always experienced tensions between its various wings and branches: between the party in Westminster and the rank and file, between the centre and the regions, between the unions and the intellectuals who formulated policy.

Debates within the party about its core aims, values and purpose will continue. It is our hope that this volume will make a positive contribution to ongoing debates within the Labour Party and the wider labour movement about our common policy directions and a future that works for the many, not the few.

We wish to dedicate this publication to our honorary president, Stan Newens, who is an embodiment of the best of Labour.

Finally, I want to thank Francis King, Duncan Bowie and Steve Cushion for much invaluable assistance.

DM

The Labour Party in Historical Perspective

Willie Thompson

Background and early years

As of mid-2018 the future prospects of the UK Labour Party are very much an en-
igma wrapped in a mystery – ironically so, for this year is the centenary of that
party's adoption of a constitution and a programme which committed it to what could
be defined as a socialist perspective and contained the famous Clause Four, 'To secure
for workers by hand and by brain the full fruits of their industry ... a basis of
common ownership' would be necessary. Up until that point, ever since the party's
formation (conventionally dated from 1900 and embodied then as the Labour Representation Committee) its only stated objective, despite membership of the Socialist International, had been to secure parliamentary representation for working people –
'workingmen' as it was stated, since of course women, working or otherwise, were
then excluded from the franchise. Ralph Miliband's classic volume of 1961, *Parliamentary Socialism*, opens with the sentence, 'Of all political parties claiming socialism as their aim, the Labour Party has always been one of the most dogmatic – not
about socialism but about the parliamentary system' – namely the system embodied
by the UK legislative authority, whose full title has always been and remains 'The
Crown in Parliament'. The phrase 'Her Majesty's Loyal Opposition' says it all.

Of all the legislative assemblies throughout Europe at the time of the Labour
Party's early years, some such as in France had revolutionary origins, and most of the
relatively democratic others imitated that model (though often reluctantly). The British one however was unique. It was a feudal institution, originally an expanded royal
court, with roots going back to the thirteenth century and with the nature of its origins
clearly exemplified by the division into Lords and Commons, not to speak of the
monarchy. Its purpose throughout the centuries has been to provide a patina of legit-
imacy for oligarchic dominance underpinned by the coercive powers of the state. The
feudal culture of deference and forelock-tugging deeply coloured the British political
system.

Still today members of Commons and Lords, likewise the Scottish parliament, are
required to affirm allegiance to the monarch and 'her heirs and successors'. (Tommy
Sheridan is said to have got round this provision by replacing, *sotto voce*, 'heirs and
successors' with 'hair and accessories'). More seriously, when in order to maintain the
imperial pretence, the Irish revolutionaries in 1922 were required to swear to the
same formula as a condition of receiving partial independence their reluctant acquies-
cence created such fury and division among their colleagues that the resulting outcome was the Irish Civil War. Immersed in such a constitutional setup it is not sur-

3

prising that the Labour Party with its parliamentary emphasis has in all its phases been readily incorporated into the oligarchic system of British rule and its leaders in the main have been all too eager to embrace its trappings and ceremonies from honours lists to Queen's speech.

Initially in past centuries that oligarchical system was secured by limiting the parliamentary electorate to individuals who were members of or safely under the thumb of the propertied authorities (though complications occurred when new types of property made their appearance in the late eighteenth and early nineteenth centuries). The demands of the mid-nineteenth century Chartists, representing the nascent industrial working class whose only property was their labour power, for a democratic rather than a propertied form of parliamentary government (despite excluding women) were therefore revolutionary demands and so of course were suppressed with severe brutality, as described by John Saville in *The British State and the Chartist Movement*.

Thereafter it became the practice of radical movements in mainland Britain, including working class ones, to operate within the boundaries of the existing monarchical and aristocratic political system (until early in the twentieth century prime ministers were as likely to sit in the House of Lords as in the Commons). The organised working class represented by the trade unions which were established in the later part of that century inclined to give their political allegiance to one faction of the ruling oligarchy, namely the Liberal Party, which appeared to be the more responsive to workers' needs – within limits and up to a point. The propertied elite were politically divided between those who resisted any change lest it endanger their property and privilege – the Tories, and those who thought some minimal change would be necessary and appropriate to protect their property and privilege from revolutionary demands – the Whigs/Liberals.

The trade unions' decision to establish the LRC at the beginning of the twentieth century with the aim of securing parliamentary representatives whose commitment was to the interests of labour, was a severely contested one, and if by that decision the nascent parliamentary Labour Party, as it was styled from 1906, had severed its organisational links with the Liberals,[1] its representatives nonetheless absorbed much of their ideological outlook, certainly on the whole to a much greater degree than they embraced the perspectives of the socialist organisations which were also involved with the new party, and certainly rejecting the revolutionary pose of the syndicalists who were at the time strong within many trade unions and despised parliamentary politics. Writing of a later phase, Henry Pelling, no friend to the left, commented in his *Short History of the Labour Party* that, 'But it is doubtful if Snowden as Chancellor of the Exchequer, actually wanted to do anything of which the most orthodox Liberal would have disapproved.'

---

[1]   Though in the general election of 1905 a Liberal-LRC electoral agreement was in place and in the subsequent parliament the labour representatives generally voted with the Liberals.

War and Aftermath

With the onset of world war beginning in 1914 the Labour Party was party to pre-war commitments as a member party of the Socialist International to oppose war if it broke out. Despite conducting mass demonstrations against war in the days before British involvement, after a further few days the Labour leadership both parliamentary and industrial had in the majority surrendered to the elite propaganda offensive, and went on to issue declarations urging their electors and British workers into the slaughterhouse (Keir Hardie and ironically Ramsay MacDonald at that time were exceptions). A few months later the leaders even joined the predatory government composed of the Liberals who had declared war and their now Tory allies. In Miliband's words, 'Like their colleagues in France, Germany and Austria, they found overwhelming the call to national identification and responded to it the more readily in order to dispel any doubt as to Labour's patriotism'. It exemplified the phenomenon that when the magic words 'national interest' are pronounced the Labour Party parliamentarians in the main, and certainly their leaders, have historically caved in as eagerly as anyone else duped by the British oligarchic elites.[2]

The Labour Party of the nineteen-twenties with its new, more socialist-appearing constitution, advancing numbers, widespread successes in local government, displacement of the Liberals as the main anti-Tory force and not least two general election successes, albeit partial ones, which put Ramsay MacDonald into Downing Street, seemed to be progressing towards inevitable hegemony in the UK and carrying through a programme which would by parliamentary means seriously alter the distribution of power and wealth in the UK – leaving outside of that picture the existence of the British Empire, to which the Labour leaders were as firmly committed as any Tory. In contrast, by the end of the thirties it was not inconceivable that the party might well be on its deathbed after bitter divisions and splits, leadership defections, successes only in some local government contexts such as the London County Council, and no more than a very minimal recovery in the general election of 1935 from its annihilation in that of 1931. All that despite the rise of left-wing sentiment throughout the country on an anti-fascist basis. So far as the latter development was concerned the attitude of the Labour leadership, even those who replaced MacDonald and his confederates after their defection, was ambiguous at best. As Miliband put it, 'But the Labour leaders of those years [were not exempt from] their own share of guilt and their own contribution to the politics of appeasement through the immunity from effective challenge they provided to the actual culprits'.

Nevertheless the Labour Party had enough of a parliamentary presence and recognised support throughout the country to be invited in 1940 to join the Churchill

---

[2]   The one significant exception, made under rank-and-file pressure, was in 1920, with parliamentary support, to refuse the Jolly George cargo ship intended to carry arms to be used against the Soviet Union and threaten wider industrial action if the government forced the issue.

wartime coalition – indeed its leaders partially determined the outcome by refusing to join a coalition under any other Conservative and the Labour leaders went on to occupy significant roles during the course of the war.

The Climax of Labourism

The Second World War certainly represented Labour's turning point through the conflict's demonstration that the hitherto despised approaches of public control, management and guidance over industry, combined with a welfare and rationing programme that saw the British population better fed than it had been during pre-war years, were essential to the country's survival and successful prosecution of the war. The enormously popular Beveridge Report of 1942 demanded the continuation of such a welfare system into the postwar years.[3] Public perception was also greatly influenced by the fact that the Soviet Union, perceived as the exemplar of undiluted socialism, was a most valued ally and the crucial instrument of Nazi defeat. In the result, though the Labour leadership favoured the

continuation of the Coalition into the postwar era, grass-roots opinion in the party obliged them to withdraw from it after the victory in 1945, precipitating a general election which resulted in a Labour landslide electoral victory that saw Churchill evicted from Downing Street and Attlee installed as premier.

The years which followed were described by Miliband as 'The Climax of Labourism', and incontestably, they were. For once, the pre-electoral promises were largely kept. Public ownership was applied to public services, from transport to coal production, to amenities such as water and power, to health and with exceptions, to education and accompanied with a government-supported municipal housing programme of unprecedented dimensions.

That however was only part of the story and the other parts were much less commendable. The greater part of the industrial economy remained in private hands (for example the civil airlines were flown by public corporations, but the planes were privately manufactured). In the areas of public ownership, (then unashamedly termed

---

[3]   Ironically, both Beveridge, and also Keynes, whose proposals for economic management had become the financial orthodoxy, were politically both Liberals.

6

'nationalisation') it was noted that the culture of top-down management was preserved and the introduction of workplace democracy not permitted. Moreover, with the Indian exception the Empire continued in existence. The banking system, with the exception of the Bank of England, remained in private hands and what are now termed 'financial services' were wholly incorporated into the private economic sector.

The last point is particularly important and relates to the key direction taken by the British economy under Labour stewardship. Prior to 1939 and the war's outbreak the UK had huge capital investments located abroad. During the war these had been drastically run down in order to pay for supplies from the USA, and in this respect the Americans, even under Roosevelt, showed no mercy until the institution of lend-lease when the reserves were exhausted.[4] It was central to the aim of Britain's financial oligarchy to rebuild these reserves and continue sterling as an international currency. Attlee's government adopted that principle without hesitation, contributing to the tremendous financial pressure under which the country found itself. In addition when the British government through its representative J M Keynes pleaded for assistance all the US would offer was a commercial loan on hard terms.

Not all the results of the 1945 victory were positive ones. It was of course the launchpad for US world hegemonic endeavours, but in addition the UK establishment elites remained convinced that the victory belonged to them and that the British Empire must continue as a superpower beside the USA and the USSR, including colonies, colonial wars and repression, which Attlee's administration conducted. Also, thanks to the publicity surrounding the patriotic role the royals played during the war, royalty worship was entrenched throughout British society and popular culture, along with continuation of the aristocratic system they headed. This remained a system which the Labour government and parliamentary Party unhesitatingly bought into; and alongside it into the British oligarchy's definition of reality and history.

This definition by the late forties included a recognition however reluctant by that oligarchy, in face of the military, industrial and financial exhaustion brought about by the war, that after all the empire was no longer what it had been. So our Establishment, with Churchill leading even though no longer in formal power, concluded that only by submitting to US ascendancy could they retain the remnants of their own former dominance. In order to remain the senior vassal to the US hegemon and maintain the pretence of bring still a 'great power' the Foreign Office mandarins, politically supported by their puppet Foreign Secretary, Ernest Bevin, insisted that the UK too must have atomic (later nuclear) weaponry, again at enormous expense and to the detriment of British social improvement. Furthermore, lubricated from 1948 by Marshall Aid, Britain had to accept integration into the US Cold War project, ramp up

---

[4]   See Robert Skidelsky's biography of Keynes, Vol 3, *John Maynard Keynes: Fighting for Britain, 1937–1946*, for an extended account.

its 'defence' expenditure, perform as an enthusiastic member of the NATO alliance and accept US military bases on its territory and in its territorial waters.

From the twenties the USA, in spite of also being a victim of the global Depression, was well on the way to becoming the world's financial hegemon, and even at that time its financial chiefs were intervening in British political affairs, refusing in 1931 to extend a loan to Ramsay MacDonald's financially embarrassed government unless it attacked the unemployed and underpaid, resulting thereafter in his surrender to them and to the Tories. By the forties the US economy had benefited greatly from war production, and its oligarchy, having by 1948 rendered the UK and most of western Europe its pensioner, aimed to extend to global proportions the hegemony it had exercised hitherto over the Caribbean and Latin America. All that involved an enormous military build-up, together with hundreds of overseas bases, accompanied with intransigent hostility to the Soviet bloc and communist China. Thus began the vassal 'special relationship', so much applauded by British establishment politicians of all parties – the sort of relationship that dogs have with lampposts.[5]

Clement Attlee

The Labour leadership, even Aneurin Bevan[6], (though he objected to some of its more invidious results) and Labour ideologists such as Anthony Crosland, eagerly embraced this outlook and adopted the Atlanticist perspective as their own (the fiercely anti-communist Hugh Dalton was kept out of the foreign secretaryship he coveted and would have suited because he was regarded as not anti-communist enough). Later the Labour deputy leader and drunkard George Brown created a scandal by his public blubbering on television over the Kennedy assassination, which did not stop him being appointed foreign secretary when Harold Wilson was prime minister.

In 1906 the Tory Leader Arthur Balfour in the wake of a Tory electoral defeat declared that no matter who was in Downing Street the great Tory party would continue to set the political agenda and effectively govern the country. He had a point. In the circumstances immediately following World War II the oligarchy could not prevent the implementation of the Labour domestic or Indian independence

---

[5] In a token demonstration of independence however, the Attlee government gave diplomatic recognition to the new communist China in spite of US refusal to do so.

[6] I was astonished to learn, that at that period the left Labour journal *Tribune*, edited by Bevan, was partly financed by the CIA, as noted by Frances Stonor Saunders in *Who Paid the Piper?: The CIA and the Cultural Cold War*, Granta, 2000.

programme but they could live with and even be quite comfortable with it. There was no significant shift in wealth, power and property during the Attlee administration, and the succeeding Tory governments, following Labour's electoral defeat in 1951 more or less continued in a similar vein in domestic and foreign policy and even continued the formal liquidation of the British Empire. Labour under Gaitskell, to be sure, opposed the Suez aggression in 1956, but so did the more intelligent Tories, not to mention the USA. Harold Wilson by contrast, with a decent parliamentary majority after 1966 was compelled by financial pressure to abandon his economic reforming programme. His one assertion of independence was to refuse to send British troops to Vietnam, contrary to US wishes – his thanks from the oligarchy was to be indicted by their secret state as a Soviet agent.

Left Surge and Debacle

During the 1970s in the wake of the 1970 electoral defeat and the unsatisfactory victories of 1974, all in the context of the Northern Ireland crisis, the final stages of the Vietnam war and the onset of the economic depression that still remains with us, a left wing current began to assert itself within the Labour Party and even to achieve organisational victories which would make the party more responsive to its member-ship and less to its establishment-orientated leaders. Tony Benn, who had disillusion-ing experience of cabinet membership, emerged as its principal spokesperson and Stuart Holland's *The Socialist Challenge* was its manifesto. It aimed to break with the traditional policies of defending at all costs sterling as an international currency, and the pretence of continuing to be a great power.

The left surge encountered its nemesis when in 1981 Benn failed in his election bid to become the party's deputy leader. The fact that this seemingly secondary event des-troyed the left challenge was indicative of the weakness of the left current of that time. Patrick Seyd has summed it up: '... concentration on political advance through ... internal structural reforms was at the expense of developing a radical programme which combined electoral credibility, practical application and popular support'.[7]

A renegade faction of the party, led by the infamous Gang of Four, had by then broken away in alarm at the prospect of the party distancing itself from the oligarch-ical Atlanticist consensus. They eventually united with the Liberals to form the Lib Dem party and though unable to win government power inflicted severe electoral de-feats on Labour to the benefit of the Tories. This led to the retraction of nearly all of the party's left advances of the seventies and early eighties[8] and eventually under the New Labour flag a complete embrace of neoliberal economics and acceptance of the Thatcherite destruction of the postwar social consensus. By comparison with Tony

---

[7]   Patrick Seyd, *The Rise and Fall of the Labour Left*, Palgrave, 1987.

[8]   See Mike Marqusee and Richard Heffernan, *Defeat from the Jaws of Victory; Inside Kinnock's Labour Party*, Verso, 1992, for an intriguing though not wholly reliable account.

Blair and his sidekick Peter Mandelson, even Ramsay MacDonald himself was a principled socialist.

Social Democracy?

The name of Social Democrats which the breakaway hijacked was itself a lie. The name was initially adopted in the nineteenth century by the Marxist-influenced parties of the continent because the term 'communist' was regarded as too provocative. Later, when following the Russian Revolution the victorious Bolsheviks of the Russian Social Democratic Labour Party renamed themselves Communists, the name of Social Democrats came to mean parties which aimed at less than revolutionary but nonetheless substantive social change through existing constitutional channels and a basic strategy of never uniting parliamentary with industrial challenge, though they might nevertheless, like the then German version from the twenties to the fifties, acknowledge Marx as a foundational influence. Even Labour Party demonstrations before the First World War often carried banners with Marx's portrait on them. The Labour Party itself prior to the Gang of Four's opportunism was happy to be counted among the social democrats, though its spokespeople normally avoided using the actual term, but might applaud existing social democratic regimes such as the Scandinavian ones.

So toxic was the Blair regime within the party, and under his premiership, within the country, that some activists opined that even the Lib Dems of that time were slightly more committed to the public services, anti-militarism and popular aspirations, and that the Blairite grip on the party was irremovable because it had administratively closed all avenues to left wing expression – these included selection procedures for local and devolved government candidates, inner-party discussion and election of officers, and not least the national conference. Ken Livingstone had to stand against the official Labour Party candidate to turn his popular support into victory in the first London mayoralty election.

To pass on to present concerns: due to a misestimate by the designers of a voting system which was actually designed to prevent this sort of thing from ever happening, the Labour Party finds itself with a leader who is actually a real social democrat. The oligarchy and its media publicists, not to mention the careerists on his own backbenches and in local government, are wetting themselves at the thought of such a person leading the Labour Party and even more at the prospect that he might be elected prime minister, and are therefore sparing no dirty trick, smear or witch-hunting initiative to get rid of him and ensure there remains no real challenge to their supremacy.

The problem with social democracy is that it stands upon capitalist foundations, with capitalism relied on to produce the material necessities and circumstances needed to implement social democracy's social programmes.[9] The nearest the UK ever got to this was the Attlee administration, but only at the cost of leaving the essential interests and props of the oligarchy untouched and with incorporation into the US empire. Even in the best of times, such as the 'golden years' of the fifties and sixties, the foundations of prosperity are insecure and the capitalist wolf in its neo-liberal fur is always waiting to show its teeth and pounce, as it did not only in the UK, assisted by that country's combined capitalist/feudal social structure and media publicists, but also in the Scandinavian social democracies where the feudal heritage had disappeared. 'Sweden needs Saab but Saab does not need Sweden,' as one unusually honest monopolist remarked.

In the face of the twenty-first century global crises both political and environmental, social democratic solutions, while they may be tried as the only accessible ones in the circumstances, will not prove to be adequate. That is something which the Labour Party will have to discover, and the public to understand; consequently much more radical approaches are necessary. What these are to be, however, is something to be discussed in a different forum.

Jeremy Corbyn at a rally in Liverpool

---

[9]   This was recognised by Anthony Crosland in *The Future of Socialism* in 1956, and he treated that as being no problem and even to be welcomed.

The Origins of Jeremy Corbyn

Graham Taylor

The election of the left-wing Jeremy Corbyn, in dramatic circumstances, as leader of the Labour Party in September, 2015, was unexpected, but not unprecedented. The party has customarily been divided into a right wing (close to Liberals and Conservatives), a left wing (close to Marxists but not Marxist) and a reformist or Social-Democratic core, and since the beginnings of the party there has been a pattern of a drift to the right interrupted by a sudden left-wing correction.

Corbyn's unpredicted elevation expressed frustration on the left at years of austerity after the world economic crisis of 2008; at Brown's failure to take over the banks or punish the bankers; at the marketisation of public services; and at the unending wars in Afghanistan, Iraq and Libya. The Labour Party in 1997-2015 had suffered a steep decline in its votes, membership, and morale. The right-wing leaders were unresponsive to protest, even to a demonstration over a million strong in 2003, and did not accept that Labour was re-elected in 2005 only because the bitterly divided Conservatives had much the same policies. Even after their defeat in the 2010 election, the right wing insisted that Labour must not deviate "one millimetre" from policies they had devised back in 1994.

The First Correction (1892)

The first correction of a stale right-wing regime predated the Labour Party itself. In the late 1880s Keir Hardie was frustrated that most 'Labour' (Lib-Lab) MPs within Gladstone's Liberal Party were failing to represent working-class interests in Parliament, although the 1884 Reform Act had enfranchised working-class voters. In 1892 Hardie, in protest, stood as an independent for West Ham South (independent, that is, of the Liberal Party) and was elected. The Independent Labour Party (ILP) was founded in Bradford in 1893, and during the 1890s it was routinely referred to in the press as 'the Labour Party'.

It is characteristic of corrections that they issue from a prior upsurge in militancy. Hardie in 1892 was washed ashore by a tide of trade union militancy in 1887-91 which had exposed the complacency of the right-wing Lib-Lab MPs, and attracted sympathy from mainstream religious and political figures - Cardinal Manning, even Gladstone - first towards the match-girls (1888) and then the dockers (1889). In 2013-15, just prior to Corbyn's elevation, there was a similar tell-tale shift in mainstream sympathy during anti-austerity campaigns over food banks, homelessness, and the plight of doctors and nurses.

Hardie's arrival at the House of Commons in 1892 met with a reaction similar to that which greeted Corbyn in 2015. Instead of addressing fundamental issues (unemployment and strikes for Hardie, austerity and wars for Corbyn), the commentators reacted by ridiculing their policies, and their clothes (Hardie's hat and Corbyn's tie). As Kenneth Morgan wrote: "Hardie's flamboyant entry into parliament, his outspoken attacks on the Queen and the royal family, his advocacy of such terrifying doctrines as socialism, feminism, pacifism, and colonial freedom all prejudiced conventional opinion against him..."[1] Morgan added that attacking Labour leaders for their clothes revealed the snobbery of their enemies: Jimmy Thomas's dinner-jacket, Harold Wilson's Gannex raincoat, Michael Foot's 'donkey jacket'.

As will be seen, the pattern is that a correction revivifies Labour, and this revivification now had positive results. The Liberals moved to the left, and adopted the Social Liberalism of Campbell-Bannerman and Lloyd George; in 1898 the ILP and the Marxist SDF won control of West Ham Council, a historic victory for British socialism; in 1900 the ILP, the SDF, the Fabians and several trade unions formed the Labour Representation Committee (LRC), an event often regarded as the foundation of the Labour Party as we know it.

The ILP became the left wing of the LRC, and its left-wing philosophy was called 'ethical socialism'. This is not to be confused with a later ethical socialism (fairness with duty) of Crosland and the German SDP. The ILP version, much influenced by Mazzini, aimed at knitting together all humanity - at an individual level by comradeliness and kindness and socially by uniting in the struggle for emancipation workers, women and ethnic groups. It was a socialism for practice in daily life, as distinct from the Fabian belief in state planning by intellectuals and the Marxist belief in

Keir Hardie

class warfare to gain state power. Hardie wrote: "Socialism, like every other problem of life, is at bottom a question of ethics or morals."[2] In 1915 the *Merthyr Pioneer* chose to announce Hardie's death by saying that the "Member for Humanity has resigned his seat."[3]

The 'socialism of humanity' did not exclude appreciation of Marxism. Hardie understood that the liberation of humanity needed economic analysis such as that by

1   Kenneth Morgan, *Labour People* (1989 edn of 1987), p. 24
2   James Keir Hardie, *Serfdom to Socialism* (2015 edn of 1907), p. 80
3   Kevin Jefferys, *Leading Labour: From Keir Hardie to Tony Blair* (1999), p. 16

Thorold Rogers and Marx. Although he relied on Philip Snowden for his economics (as Corbyn does on John McDonnell), he was much influenced by Marx. Indeed the term, 'ethical socialism', was first used, pejoratively, by Rosa Luxemburg against the Marxism of Eduard Bernstein who Hardie knew and admired. Hardie also admired the British Marxist, William Morris. As John Callow wrote, anyone familiar with Marx will recognise him in Hardie's writings.[4] And Maxton held Hardie "more Marxist than those who paid deference to Marxist theories".[5]

In 1906 the ILP's aim of electing a strong body of working-class MPs to Parliament was achieved. The 29 MPs called themselves the 'Labour Party' and elected Hardie as Chair. Yet the 'Labour Party (LRC)' was still only a federation. Within the LRC the 'Labour Party (ILP)' acted as the guardian of socialism since, as Hardie averred, the ILP was "created for the purpose of realising socialism" and winning seats in Parliament was only a means to that end.[6] This attitude shaped the outlook of the Labour left, and it reignited the Labour Party from cold ashes in 1914, 1932, 1960, 1972, 1980 and 2015.

The Second Correction (1914)

By 1910 the Labour Party (LRC) had drifted back to the right. The MPs were regularly voting with the Liberals. Like the pigs in Orwell's *Animal Farm*, they had reverted to the Lib-Lab posture the ILP was founded to combat. At the ILP conference Hardie reported, sadly: "The Labour Party has almost ceased to exist." As MacDonald explained in *The Socialist Movement* (1911): the Labour Party did not have a philosophy as the ILP did; It was not socialist, whereas the ILP was; Labour was just a combination of socialist and trade union bodies "for immediate practical work".[7] At the skating rink in Merthyr Tydfil in 1912 Hardie said "the ILP's ultimate objective remained revolution, not merely reform" but many trade unionists had joined Labour without a socialist perspective.[8] In 1910 'General Gribble', leader of the Raunds bootmakers, put it far less politely: "What are we paying to send men of our own class to Parliament for? Is it to represent our views, our aims, our aspirations, or to make openings for some of the sharp ones to get into office?"[9]

Once again, as in 1887-91, a militant movement from below heralded a corrective break. In 1910-14 strikes broke out in mines, in docks and on railways, culminating in the Dublin lock-out of 1913. At the same time the suffragettes were campaigning for the vote, and strikes by working-class women led by Mary Macarthur scored un-

4   John Callow, Introduction to *From Serfdom to Socialism* by Keir Hardie (2015 edn of 1907), pp. 26-28.
5   Caroline Benn, *Keir Hardie* (1992), p. 260
6   Pauline Bryan (ed), *What Would Keir Hardie Say?* (2015), p. 32
7   Kevin Jefferys, *Leading Labour: From Keir Hardie to Tony Blair* (1999), p. 27
8   Kenneth Morgan, *Keir Hardie: Radical and Socialist* (1997 edn of 1975), p. 253
9   Graham Taylor, *Ada Salter: Pioneer of Ethical Socialism* (2016), p. 121

precedented victories, as in the Bermondsey Uprising. The ILP was involved in all of them, as well as in campaigns, crucially, to stop the fast approaching war.

The second correction may be dated to the outbreak of war in August, 1914. Labour (LRC) supported the war but the ILP did not. MacDonald, whose base was in the ILP, not in the unions, was obliged to resign as Chair of the Labour Party. This stand later brought Labour rewards, as did all the corrections. After 1918, as returning soldiers cheered the anti-war candidates at meetings, the public's attitude to the war changed. In 1922 ILP candidates won many seats and MacDonald, an anti-war icon with moral authority, became the first 'leader' of the Labour Party. In 1924 he became first Labour Prime Minister. Like Corbyn, he owed his success, at least in part, to an ethical stance against war.

The ILP was the only British party to oppose the war. The Labour Party joined the Liberals and Conservatives in supporting it, and the Marxist British Socialist Party (successor to the SDF and SDP) first wavered, then split. The ILP was also one of the few parties in Europe to oppose the war, and congratulations poured into the ILP offices from Rosa Luxemburg, Karl Liebknecht and Clara Zetkin. Even Lenin was impressed. It was generally agreed that, because of the ILP, the summer of 1914 was British socialism's finest hour.

Keith Laybourn, although conceding that the ILP reaffirmed its opposition to the war at its Norwich conference in 1915, has pointed to the disintegration of the ILP's opposition to the war at local level, even in Bradford, after 1915. He says the majority of the ILP felt obliged, in the end, to be "patriotic" and "fight for their country"[10] But this underestimates the cruel intensity of the intimidation. ILP members were beaten up in the street; they lost their jobs; buildings in which they were speaking were set alight; and, as COs, some even suffered torture.[11] Even one third of eligible Quakers eventually cracked up and agreed to enlist.

It is the opposite question which is more interesting: why was the British ILP able to stick to its anti-war principles when most left-wing parties, including the Marxist German SPD, did not? The Marxist parties capitulated, said Alexandra Kollontai, because they failed to understand "the moral influence of the old bourgeois world on the mood of the populace."[12] But the ILP, she pointed out, was based on ethics, not only self-interest. Ethical socialism recognised that, as well as the material concerns of life, humanity also had moral, cultural and social concerns. This was to be developed by Gramsci later, when he showed that in Western Europe the left needed to win 'hegemony', not just pay rises and votes.

---

10 Keith Laybourn in *Stop the First World War!* (SHS Occasional Publication, 2016), pp. 4-24
11 Graham Taylor, *Ada Salter: Pioneer of Ethical Socialism* (2016), pp. 138-40, p. 146, p. 180
12 Alexandra Kollontai, *Selected Articles and Speeches* (1984), p. 67

Understanding this ethical, and hegemonic, element in the early Labour Party is important for understanding Corbyn. Not only was he able to withstand intense pressure to resign in 2015-16, to the astonishment of a cynical political class, but his principled stand in the face of daily abuse attracted wide admiration, and an increase in his vote.

The ILP was also victorious in domestic affairs. They had campaigned since the 1890s for adult suffrage (including suffrage for women) and for state intervention on social questions (a welfare state). Already, from 1906, the presence of 29 Labour MPs in Parliament made the Liberal Party fear for its future and Lloyd George introduced his 'People's Budget' in 1909, raising taxes to pay for state assistance to pensioners, the sick and the unemployed. It was Britain's first, though very basic, welfare state. When in 1918 all men and 40% of women received the vote (granted on equal terms in 1928), the ILP's programme was at last implemented, despite a century of fierce opposition to both democracy and welfare from Conservatives and many Liberals.

Thus, in the two corrections of 1892 and 1914, the Labour left (in this case the ILP) ran up a flag of defiance that re-energised the Labour ranks, just as Corbyn did in 2015, and this eventually brought long-term gains of historic proportions.

The Third Correction (1932)

After the short-lived 1924 government the Labour Party once again moved to the right, and the second minority government (1929-31) saw close Lib-Lab co-operation. The argument that nothing very radical could be done with a minority government was a powerful one in 1924. At the same time dissent in the party, particularly from Communists and women, was under attack.[13] The ILP stood against all this, supporting women candidates, the arrested Communists and the General Strike of 1926, but to no avail.

George Lansbury

The most right-wing move was yet to come. In 1931 a world economic crisis struck home. MacDonald, instead of resigning, agreed after an interview with King George to accept, on behalf of the labour movement he represented, mass unemployment and austerity. He was duly expelled from the party as a traitor but at the subsequent general election, led by the 'moderate' Arthur Henderson, Labour was almost wiped out.

---

13 Andrew Thorpe, *A History of the British Labour Party* (2008 edn of 1997)

This led to the third correction. Again, the left shift emerged from a background of intense protest. Hunger marches organised by the Communist Party against mass unemployment climaxed in the national hunger march of 1932, which mobilised 100,000 people in London and caused the biggest police deployment since 1848. Unemployment had reached 2.75 million. In the eye of this storm Labour chose as leader of the party, George Lansbury, an old ILP comrade of Hardie. As with Corbyn, this was astonishing after a decade of Labour 'moderation'. But, like MacDonald, Lansbury had moral authority derived from opposing the 1914 war. It is as if the Labour Party, in a crisis as in 2015, suddenly remembers the ethical purpose for which it was founded. Some claim that Lansbury now saved the Labour Party. It could have just aped the MacDonald government, but instead Lansbury promoted the radical plans later implemented by the Attlee government of 1945.

The Lansbury correction gained immediate rewards in municipal elections - the meat and drink of ethical socialism. In 1934 Labour won control of London, and in the 1935 general election Labour gained 154 seats. Postgate wrote that the policies of Attlee's government were influenced by no one more than Lansbury.[14] As with Corbyn later, the huge vote for Labour in 1945 was due to "a flood of previous non-voters and of first-time voters."[15]

The Fourth Correction (1960)

In 1951 Attlee was defeated, but not overwhelmingly. Labour received more votes than the Conservatives and still had a radical feel. But, after 1951, Attlee continued to move to the right and was succeeded as leader in 1955 by Gaitskell, further right still. By 1959-60 the majority of Labour supporters were unable to recognise the difference between the policies of the main parties.[16] This was the same scenario that lent lustre to Hardie in 1892, the ILP in 1914, Lansbury in 1932, and Corbyn in 2015.

As with the previous corrections, this one was heralded by an explosion of militancy from below (1889, 1912, 1926). In 1957 strikes in shipbuilding and engineering produced the most serious crisis in industrial relations since the General Strike. In 1957, too, a 'New Left' began to challenge the right. By 1960 the *New Left Review* was aiming for a movement based on 'socialist humanism'. Edward Thompson said this was a "moral standpoint" that rejected the twin "philistinisms" of Stalinism and Social Democracy.[17] Like the ILP's ethical socialism it was based on one humanity and the power of universal reason.

The fourth correction came, however, not from the strikes but from the peace movement. In 1958 the Campaign for Nuclear Disarmament (CND) was launched

---

14 Raymond Postgate, *The Life of George Lansbury* (1951), p. 294
15 Eric Hobsbawm in Jacques & Mulhern (ed): *The Forward March of Labour Halted?* (1981), p. 175n
16 Ralph Miliband, *Parliamentary Socialism* (1972 edn of 1961), pp. 337-39
17 Madeleine Davis in Howell, Kirby & Morgan (ed): *John Saville, Commitment and History* (2011), p. 37

and it was CND which won a vote at Labour Party Conference in 1960 that shattered the cross-party consensus nurtured by the Labour right. The formation shortly afterwards of the 'Committee of 100' by Bertrand Russell made the break decisive. The Committee advocated non-violent direct action on the streets and, like the ILP, had a hegemonic profile, enlisting film directors, art critics, playwrights, musicians and poets to the cause.

By this time it was no longer the ILP but the Tribune group of MPs who represented the Labour left. In 1932 the ILP had disaffiliated from Labour and been replaced on the left by the Socialist League, which attracted former ILP members such as Cripps, Attlee, Salter and Cole, as well as Murphy from the CPGB. Although eventually shut down by the party in 1937, the Socialist League left behind as a gift to the next generation a left periodical, *Tribune*. It was now an alliance between CND and those MPs who supported *Tribune* that led the charge in 1960.

As before, this correction led to a re-energisation and Harold Wilson, Labour's next leader in 1963, although not a left-winger, was a left reformist. In the 1964 election Wilson used left-wing language, attacking commercialism, speculators and the aristocracy. He offered a left-wing manifesto: a national economic plan, public ownership of the private monopolies (steel, water), the right to trade union representation, comprehensive schools, equal pay for equal work, support for an Arts Council, and laws against racial discrimination. Just as MacDonald gained in moral authority on account of his anti-war stand in 1914, so Wilson gained by his stand of 1951 in defence of the NHS against the claims of war expenditure. In his 1962 conference speech, Wilson even tried on the mantle of ethical socialism: "The Labour Party is a moral crusade or it is nothing."

The result was a great reforming government, comparable to those of Gladstone, Lloyd George and Attlee, although that was not recognised at the time by the socialists for whom feminism, anti-racism and humanitarianism were subsidiary questions. In 1965 the TUC had called on government to implement equal pay and equal opportunity for women and in 1968 militant action by Ford's women sewing machinists triggered, via Barbara Castle, the Equal Pay Act of 1970. Accompanying this historic advance for working-class women, the 1967 Sexual Offences Act partly decriminalised homosexuality and an Abortion Act in 1967 legalised abortion. In 1969 the establishment of the Open University democratised access to higher education, and capital punishment was ended for nearly all offences. Wilson also supported film-making and the arts, kept out of the Vietnam War, and ended Britain's 'East of Suez' imperialism.[18] Without the 1960 correction the Gaitskellites might have remained in place, unelectable forever.

---

18 Anne Perkins, 'Labour Needs To Rethink Harold Wilson's Legacy' (*Guardian*, 20.03.2016)

The Fifth Correction (1972)

In 1966, after winning a second election with a huge vote for Labour, Wilson was beset by economic crisis and the government moved to the right. In 1967 the pound was devalued, and there were spending cuts to the NHS, education and housing. Unemployment soared above one million while party membership slumped. In 1969 the controversial white paper, *In Place of Strife,* proposing reform of trade unions, divided the Cabinet and in 1970 Labour lost the general election they were expected to win.

The upsurge that now ensued once again originated outside Parliament, with trade unions and social movements. There were passionate demonstrations against the Vietnam War. In 1971 the first demonstrations by the Women's Liberation Movement took place. There were spectacular campaigns over homelessness, such as the occupation in London of an empty skyscraper, Centre Point, in 1974.

Strike for the Pentonville Five

The most serious 'uprising' came from the trade union movement. A full-scale miners' strike began in 1972 and later in the year the Pentonville Five dockworkers were released from prison after the TUC, astonishingly, threatened to call the first general strike since 1926. In 1973 three million trade unionists protested on the streets against the Industrial Relations Act. The labour unrest of 1970-74 "dwarfed its predecessor of 1910-14 in terms of its daring, its comprehensiveness and its success".[19]

The fifth correction may be dated to the Labour Party Conference of 1972. Subsequently, *Labour's Programme for Britain* (1973), was hailed by Michael Foot as "the finest Socialist Programme I have seen in my lifetime". Famously, Labour's radical manifesto of February, 1974, promised "a fundamental and irreversible shift in the balance of power and wealth in favour of working people". Labour would eliminate by law all discrimination against women and racial minorities, as well as introducing disability benefits, free family planning, nursery education, and the final end of selective education. After election in 1974 Labour passed the Health and Safety at

---

19 Royden Harrison in Jacques & Mulhern (ed): *The Forward March of Labour Halted?* (1981), p. 55

Work Act (which saved many lives), the 1975 Sex Discrimination Act (promoting equal opportunities at work), the 1975 Employment Protection Act (which included maternity leave) and the 1976 Race Relations Act (against racial discrimination). Thus the correction of 1972 had reversed Labour's right-wing drift, won two elections, and brought about radical legislative benefits all within four years.

The Sixth Correction (1980)

In the aftermath of the oil crisis in 1973 another economic recession occurred in 1975 and once more the right of the party regained dominance. In 1976 the government borrowed from the IMF, who imposed strict conditions of austerity on the UK, and this curbed state expenditure on further left-wing projects. Finally, in 1977 Callaghan made a pact with the Liberals, in order to stay in power, thus ending any hope of a (peaceful) socialist revolution which some on the left had dreamed of during the correction of 1972-74.

It was not just the flagging economy that was dragging Labour to the right but a change in the structure of society. In 1978 Eric Hobsbawm wrote an article in *Marxism Today*, the innovative left-wing journal edited by Martin Jacques, called *The Forward March of Labour Halted?*. Britain's foremost Marxist historian analysed deindustrialisation and evidenced the decline of the manual working class and the labour movement since 1951. It was later generally agreed that his analysis was correct,[20] although the conclusions he drew were hotly disputed. Indeed, the situation was more serious than Hobsbawm thought. By the 1970s globalisation was eroding the viability of Social Democracy and Communism, both of which relied on a centralised nation-state in control of a national economy.

In 1980 came the sixth correction, prepared in 1977-79 by an upsurge of trade union and social militancy. The correction took political shape when left reformist, Michael Foot, was elected Labour Party leader with the support of the left. However, this time was different. The unions did not attract the public sympathy they had in 1972 and the correction did not bring the usual gains to the Labour cause. Hobsbawm's pessimism was justified. Instead came a serious right-wing backlash. In 1981 four leading figures from the right broke away from the Labour Party and founded the Social Democratic Party (SDP). In alliance with the Liberals, they diverted millions of votes from Labour. Unsurprisingly, Labour was defeated in the elections of 1983, 1987 and 1992.

Tony Benn, the de facto leader of the Labour left, was aware of the three corrections since Attlee (1960, 1972, 1980), although he did not call them 'corrections' but three 'waves' of struggle against 'revisionism', and he dated them to 1959, the late

---

20 Robin Blackburn in Jacques & Mulhern (ed): *The Forward March of Labour Halted?* (1981), p. 160

1960s, and 1979-80.[21] What he did not appreciate was that this wave was not going to work its usual magic. The breakaway by the SDP, dividing the Labour vote, was going to handicap Labour for well over a decade.[22] More profoundly, the combination of financialisation, deindustrialisation and globalisation was the biggest transformation of British capitalism since the advent of the Industrial Revolution. Even if a Labour government had been elected in the 1980s it would not have been able to resurrect a Social-Democratic programme of central planning any more than Gorbachev was able to breathe new life into Communism. Henceforth the left would have to forsake notions of a superior Fabian elite, or a vanguard party, handing down doctrines, strategies or central planning from on high to social movements below.[23]

It was fitting, therefore, that the revival of Labour after the 1980 correction started with municipal socialism. It was no longer possible to impose 'socialism' by directives from the state, but local government could be more hegemonic and 'garden' social values as they sprouted up organically from below. Thus, in the 1980s left-wingers took control of many local councils across the country and tried to unite together, in some 'rainbow coalition', all the social movements of women, workers, ethnic minorities, gays and greens. For their pains they were dubbed by the press as 'loony-left councils'. Two of the leading 'loony-left councillors' were Ken Livingstone elected in 1987 as an MP in Brent and Jeremy Corbyn elected in 1983 as an MP in Islington. Livingstone had become the leader of the Greater London Council in 1981 and in 2000 and 2004 he was elected Mayor of London. He was the most successful left-wing politician of the day, before Corbyn's victory in 2015.

Livingstone and Corbyn were just one part of a new socialist movement in the 1980s that like the old ILP was rooted, simultaneously, both in local community and global humanity. Symbolised, perhaps, by the Live Aid concert of 1985, it appealed to common humanity and human rights, encouraging left hegemony not from the top down but from the grass roots upwards. The arrival of the Green Party on the political scene, with its concern for the whole planet, reinforced the same perspective. Such an outlook was not far from the ILP's socialism in which the Labour Party had been grounded - the ILP was not so much a party as "a way of life" said Brockway.[24] That approach had been marginalised during the Cold War by (Fabian) Social Democracy and Soviet Communism but, with their demise, it now re-emerged. In the 1960s Raymond Williams had bemoaned its loss, and "blamed this not only on the Fabians' imposition of a utilitarian outlook but also on the uncompromising economism of the Marxists who opposed them."[25] However, by the end of the 1980s, the 'socialism of

21 Tony Benn in Jacques & Mulhern (ed): *The Forward March of Labour Halted?* (1981), pp. 81-82
22 Richard Seymour, *The Strange Rebirth of Radical Politics* (2017 edn of 2016), p. 311.
23 Graham Taylor in *Politics and Power: New Perspectives on Socialist Politics* (1980), pp. 149-163
24 Fenner Brockway, *Towards Tomorrow* (1977), p. 24
25 Madeleine Davis in Callaghan, Fielding & Ludlam (ed): *Interpreting the Labour Party* (2003), p. 47

humanity' was back, still playing music, still adamant for its principles, but wearing new clothes.

The recovery of Labour at national level was of a different nature. Severely damaged by the SDP defections it was not until 1997 that Labour won its next election and, by then, it had in Tony Blair a right-wing leader. Nonetheless the 1997 victory still obeyed the rule that Labour cannot be elected (as opposed to re-elected) without a radical programme. Blair's programme included legislation on human rights; child care; devolution in Scotland, Wales and London; abolition of the House of Lords; consideration of Proportional Representation; a Freedom of Information Act; a minimum wage; and greatly increased spending on health and education. Blair claimed it was the biggest programme of constitutional reform ever undertaken in a democracy. However, the policies were not from Blair's New Labour, but inherited from Smith, Kinnock and Foot. Devolution and abolition of the Lords dated back to Hardie. Though not enamoured of New Labour, the left was nonetheless enthusiastic for this programme. Corbyn named as his "proudest moment in politics" cycling home after voting for the minimum wage under Blair's leadership in 1998.[26]

The Seventh Correction (2015)

Disillusionment with Blair was fairly swift, despite his undoubted gifts as a communicator. Not only had he felt obliged to dilute several policies that were promised in 1997 but from 2001 his own New Labour policies started to appear and these proved unsatisfactory to many Labour voters, especially those on the left uneasy about the marketisation of public services and the proliferation of Private Finance Initiatives. In the 2001 general election there was a drop in Labour's vote of nearly three million and turnout plunged below 60%. By the 2010 election, after two more terms of New Labour, Labour's vote had crashed to its lowest level since 1918, at only 29%, and that barely shifted in 2015.

Unease in the party deepened under Brown since ethical questions raised about the Iraq War and the use of torture (by rendition) were multiplied by the banking crisis of 2008 and the crisis over MPs' expenses in 2009. Within the party New Labour tried to keep the left at bay by restricting political debate, locally and at conference, but this depoliticised not only MPs but also local councillors, many of whom came to regard themselves not as political representatives, but only as administrators.[27]

Nonetheless, the economic crisis of 2008 opened up a wide-ranging cultural and ethical debate. Whereas in the 1950s debate on the left was conducted in the collectivist terms of state and class, debate in the 21st century revolved around either self-interest and identity or ethical appeals to our common humanity against the divisions

---

26 Rosa Prince, *Comrade Corbyn* (2016), p. 144
27 Peter Latham, *Who Stole the Town Hall?* (2017), p. 154

of class, sex and race. In 2009 *The Spirit Level* by Kate Pickett and Richard Wilkinson responded to the economic crisis by initiating a debate about equality. It was followed by *Capital in the Twenty-First Century* (2013) by Thomas Piketty, and books by Danny Dorllng and Owen Jones. For the first time, such debates were amplified on the social media through Facebook and Twitter, short-circuiting the press.

The literary critic, Terry Eagleton, who had oscillated previously between Catholic ethics and Althusserian Marxism, now arrived at an 'ethical Marxism', after realising that ethics and politics are "not separate spheres but different viewpoints on the same object..."[28] He found in Marx that economic analysis was always interwoven with ethical passion. In *Why Marx was Right* (2011) he argued: "In line with his Judaic legacy, Marx was a strenuously moral thinker"[29]. Similarly, Naomi Klein identified a necessary linkage between green and ethical discussion (connected since the fate of the planet was also the fate of humanity). She echoed Kollontai in warning political parties that it was not possible in a democracy to win the argument on climate change by appealing to self-interest alone. They must also forge alliances around "a moral imperative".[30]

From 2013 a new upsurge began. Protests and strikes, notably by doctors and nurses, but also by other employees such as railway workers, proliferated in the next few years. The upsurge may be dated precisely to February, 2013, when the People's Assembly against Austerity was launched. Its initial supporters included Tony Benn, Jeremy Corbyn, John McDonnell, Caroline Lucas, and leading trade unionists. Reflecting an ethical sense of injustice at the burden being imposed on lower and middle income groups by the banking crisis of 2008, its branches soon spread across the country.

Jeremy Corbyn was elected leader of the Labour Party in September, 2015. After Labour's two successive election defeats, first under the right-wing Gordon Brown in 2010 and then under the insufficiently reformist Ed Miliband in 2015, the Corbyn correction re-energised the party. His victory stunned the press and shocked the stalwarts of New Labour who had convinced themselves that "non-voters do not vote" and were therefore amazed to find that a 'non-voting' younger generation who chanted Corbyn's name at music festivals did, after all, vote. They had found something to vote for.

Corbyn won because it was felt that he hoisted a bright flag of honesty and principle above the desolate mud-flats of double-talk and triangulation. It was agreed that Corbyn, on his bike going to tend his allotment, was not a synthetic politician but 'authentic'. Researchers discovered that even at school he had been driven by "a very

---

28 Terry Eagleton, *Trouble with Strangers: A Study of Ethics* (2008), p. 316
29 Terry Eagleton, *Why Marx was Right* (2011), p. 158
30 Naomi Klein, *Speech to Labour Party Conference* (2017)

moral sense of what was right for society". When he became a vegetarian it was for ethical reasons ("I got attached to the pigs").[31] During the expenses scandal of 2009 Corbyn had claimed the smallest expenses of any MP. Corbyn consciously looked back to the left Labour tradition, revering not only Benn and Bevan but Lansbury and Hardie. His message was an ethical socialism: "Corbyn appealed for a new type of society where, 'we each care for all, everybody caring for everybody else: I think it's called socialism'."[32] To this end he often ended a speech by calling for action "together". 'Together' was a key word in his political vocabulary. Quoting Rachel Shabi on how he was "binding together" groups divided by "rampant individualism", Mark Perryman in *The Corbyn Effect* said: "None of this would appear either new or all that threatening to those steeped in the Labour tradition of Keir Hardie and Ellen Wilkinson..."[33]

For any Labour leader to win power they must, given the absence of media support, exert ethical authority. MacDonald and Attlee exercised such authority because their opponents had taken the country into war, unnecessarily it was thought. In 1964 Wilson could refer to his anti-war stand of 1951, and turn the plight of the scandal-hit Macmillan government into an ethical indictment by attacking a decadent ruling class. Even Blair was able to take the high moral ground after the turpitude of Major's MPs in the cash-for-questions affair. But Corbyn did not have to talk up his ethics. He had voted against all three disastrous wars (Afghanistan, Iraq and Libya) and from the start he had opposed austerity.

The Corbyn correction led to a dramatic revival in Labour's fortunes. In 2015 membership was down to 221,247 but by July, 2016, it was 515,000. In the 2017 general election the Labour vote share rose from 30.4% in 2015 to 40.0%. This rise of 9.6% was the biggest jump in vote share for Labour since 1945. Not only that but in Parliament Corbyn forced policy retreats on the May government with regard to tax credits, cuts in disability benefits, and the Saudi prisons contract. His only problem was that he was constantly under attack from the right wing MPs of his own party, even during the 2017 election campaign, which Labour might otherwise have won. As with the SDP in 1981, the Labour right preferred a Labour defeat to victory under a left Labour leader.

Nobody can predict how the Labour Party will fare after the correction of 2015. The history of such 'lurches to the left' (the media's term for what are here described as 'corrections') does show, however, that none of the left-wing prophets became a Prime Minister - neither Hardie, nor Lansbury, nor Bevan, nor Benn - nor did any of

31 Rosa Prince, *Comrade Corbyn* (2016), p. 34 and p. 39
32 Richard Seymour, *The Strange Rebirth of Radical Politics* (2017 edn of 2016), p. 20
33 Mark Perryman, *The Corbyn Effect* (2017), p. 23

the left-wing 'parties within the party' (the ILP, the Socialist League, the Tribune Group) exercise power. What happens is that a subsequent Prime Minister introduces some, but only some, of the policies that a prophet has campaigned for. Instead of a full-blown socialism the prophets are rewarded only with radical reforms - which may be universal suffrage or the welfare state - but these are enough to secure them the gratitude of posterity. Acknowledgement is granted also to the Prime Ministers who, for all their faults, did the decent thing. Not only are John Stuart Mill and the Chartists honoured but also Gladstone and Lloyd George.

Corbyn was, from the beginning, unlikely to become Prime Minister. Nothing is impossible of course - over Brexit the Conservatives may, for example, split. But what is more likely, from the history, is that in the 2020s there will emerge a Labour Prime Minister who will be able to implement 'the best of Corbyn', and make a lasting contribution to social progress, just as happened after previous corrections. And, of course, it is not beyond possibility that one day some such correction may achieve Corbyn's dream of a socialist society.

Tony Benn

The Rising Sun of Socialism: The emergence of the Labour Movement in the textile belt of the West Riding of Yorkshire 1890-1914

Keith Laybourn

It was E P Thompson, in his seminal article 'Homage to Tom Maguire' who, in 1960, reminded us of the value of provincial history at a time when historians were still focussing upon national events.[1] What he sought was the fusion of local and national history which would permit us to gain a fuller picture of why the radical politics of the North gave rise to the emergence of the socialist organisation, the Independent Labour Party. He stressed that the ILP emerged in the provinces of the North, emphasised the importance of the West Riding of Yorkshire in its growth, stressed that whilst the Manningham Mills strike is accredited with the Labour breakthrough, that this was an event which owed much to other strikes and other developments, the work of 'gifted propagandists and trade unionists' such as the Leeds-Irish photographer Tom Maguire.[2] Yet he recognised that no individual alone was responsible for this change and emphasised that to create a movement which was prepared to break with the past there had to be something wider, indeed it had to be 'the product of a community'.[3]

The textile district of the West Riding was a distinctive community which, for a variety of reasons, took rapidly to the new independent Labour cause. From its early successes in winning municipal and local seats in the Colne Valley, Bradford and Halifax in the early 1890s it developed to win an increasing number of municipal seats, more than doubling its local representation from 89 (47 municipal) representatives in 1906 to 189 (85 municipal) in 1913, the real breakthrough coming from about 1909 onwards. Up to that time the ILP had challenged the Liberals in their parliamentary seats with candidates such as Ben Tillett (Bradford West 1892, 1895), John Lister I (Halifax, 1893 & 1895), Tom Mann (Colne Valley, 1895), Keir Hardie (Bradford East, 1896) and H Russell Smart (Huddersfield, 1895). In the 1906 general election, however, the local independent Labour movement had developed to the point of securing three MPs (Fred Jowett, James Parker and James O'Grady) in the 1906 general election and, briefly four from 1907 to 1910, when Victor Grayson was returned for Colne Valley. Until 1906 the ILP had been a party of the municipality in West Yorkshire but thereafter it was a party also of national politics and its horizons moved towards national perspectives.

---

1   E P Thompson, 'Homage to Tom Maguire' in A Briggs and J Saville (eds), *Essays in Labour History* (London, 1960), p. 267.
2   Thompson, 'Maguire', p. 279.
3   Thompson, 'Maguire', p. 279.

The growth of the movement was seen in the success of *The Clarion, Labour Leader* and the *Yorkshire Factory Times* in the district, the last of these serving the textile workers of the district and bringing together Ben Turner, Allen Gee, W H Drew and James Bartley as contributors. Eventually by 1914 there were three local ILP papers – the *Bradford Pioneer, The Leeds Weekly Citizen* and *The Worker* (Huddersfield) although there had been many other less successful ones such as *Demos, The Labour Weekly* and *Forward*, which ran successfully throughout the Edwardian years.

There was great pride in these achievements and at the 1914 Easter Conference of the ILP, partly held in St George's Hall, Bradford, J H Palin (president of the Amalgamated Society of Railway Servants at the time of Taff Vale) stated that:

> *Of ordinary historical association, Bradford has none. In Domesday book it was described as a waste and successive periods of capitalist exploitation have done little to improve it. The history of Bradford will very largely be the history of the ILP.*[4]

Although this statement was clearly exaggerated it did raise the question why the ILP had emerged so powerfully in the textile district of the West Riding of Yorkshire. Why was there so much pride in the achievements of the ILP and the broader Labour movement in Bradford and the textile belt of the West Riding of Yorkshire.? Why was it that of the 339 delegates from 244 branches of the ILP who attended the 1914 conference that there were 52 representatives for the 24 West Yorkshire branches – 15 from Bradford alone? Why such success?

The answer, for such local, municipal and parliamentary success is, I would suggest, based upon a firm radical base which was evolving as a result of industrial changes and adapting social values. There was reflected in an immense number of interlocking and overlapping networks which created a sub-culture which provided the basis, the core, for the broader general support which came from the trade union movement – from the skilled trade unionists, threatened with industrial change, just as much as the previously unorganised unskilled and semi-skilled trade unionists. Both factors – a core of socialist support with interlocking and overlapping connections and the more general support of trade unionism were vital to the growth of the ILP in West Yorkshire and to the emergence of a powerful LRC/Labour Party in the twentieth century. What linked them, although not necessarily in a direct sense, was the willingness of the ILP and the new socialist organisation, to adapt to the new radical environment which allowed more people (after changes in 1884 and 1894) to vote for a programme of measures (housing, night-soil collection, reductions in the working day and 6d per hour and 48 hours for municipal workers etc.) which emerged before the formation of the National ILP in January 1893 and through its

4   *Yorkshire Observer Budget*, 11 April 1914.

later programmes. One is reminded here of the comment from Wilfred Whiteley, of Huddersfield and Colne Valley, that he '...spouted socialism but was returned on the issue of privy middens'. In addition, the comment of Fred Jowett, the first Labour MP for Bradford in 1906, who acknowledged, in his book *The Socialist and the City* (London, ILP, 1907) that the 'socialist could not run ahead of the will of the municipal voter." Indeed, here was a belief held by Jowett, and indeed the later Labour leader George Lansbury, that social measures could come from the working class running their own affairs in their own community in contrast to the ideas of Ramsay MacDonald and the Fabians who thought that they would come through the state.

The national debate into which Labour's political growth in the West Yorkshire area fits can be easily summarised. In essence it is an argument between those historians who maintain that Labour's growth was becoming inevitable before the Great War, as it chipped away at Liberal progressive strength, and those who maintain that the Labour Party's emergence owes much to the division of the Liberal Party and the destruction of its shibboleths during the Great War. On the one hand, there is George Dangerfield, Henry Pelling and Ross McKibbin, maintaining that Labour's capture of trade union support before the war was vital and, on the other, there is Trevor Wilson, P F Clarke, Chris Cook and many others, who focus upon the deleterious impact of the Great War on the Liberal Party. They debate the influence of New Liberalism, the impact of the restricted parliamentary franchise, local evidence and trade-union support.[5]

An alternative, third line, between these two arguments put forward by Bill Lancaster, who favours the first view, suggests that a more regional approach is desirable and that there may be differences in independent Labour growth and Liberal decline, from area to area.[6] David Howell and Duncan Tanner have adopted similar approaches, although with a different emphasis.

Although I generally support the view that Labour was making significant headway before 1914, I would accept that there was immense regional variation. In some regions there were good reasons for Labour's growth and in others there were good reasons why its growth was arrested. For instance, the Black Country was slower to develop as a Labour heartland than the textile district of the West Riding (West Yorkshire), perhaps because its trade unions were more tied up with the Liberals and the presence of a powerful Unionist tradition. In contrast the textile district of the West

5   Keith Laybourn, 'The Rise of Labour and the Decline of Liberalism: The State of the Debate', *History*, Vol. 80, No, 259, June 1995,pp.207-226; George Dangerfield, *The Strange Death of Liberal England* (London, 1966); Henry Pelling, *The Origins of the Labour Party* (London, 1954); Ross McKibbin, *The Evolution of the Labour Party* (Oxford, 1974); Keith Laybourn and Jack Reynolds, *Liberalism and the Rise of Labour 1890-1918* (Sussex, 1984); Trevor Wilson, *The Downfall of the Liberal Party 1914-1935* (London, 1966); David James, Tony Jowitt and Keith Laybourn, *The Centennial History of the Labour Party* (Halifax, 1992), and many others.
6   Bill Lancaster, 'The Rise of Labour', *Labour History Review*, lvii (1992), 98, and Bill Lancaster, *Radicalism, Cooperation and Socialism: Leicester Working-Class Politics 1860-1906* (Leicester, 1987).

Riding was at the forefront of Labour's growth. Was its growth because of (1) social-ist activists, something which Thompson placed some emphasis upon? Was it because of the accommodation of the working classes in West Yorkshire to (2) labourist rather than overtly socialist or Marxist perspectives, or was it because of the continuing contribution of (3) trade unionism to the emerging radical and socialist perspective. Or (4) should we look at why some prominent middle-class Liberals were estranged from the emerging socialist emphasis of the new movement in the late nineteenth century?

West Yorkshire Developments

Between 1890 and 1914 the independent Labour movement developed rapidly in West Yorkshire. The Bradford Labour Union was formed in May 1891 and had ac-quired more than 2,000 members, 19 clubs, and two councillors, by early 1893. It suffered difficulties in the mid-1890s but still had a hard-core of 1,600 ILP members in 1914. The Halifax Labour movement occasionally had up to 800 members but more generally about 600 on the eve of the Great War. Colne Valley Labour Union/ League and their branches were less stable. Although there were around 300 members in the mid-1890s this figure fell to about 235 in 1899, 83 or so in 1900 before recov-ering to 122 in 1902.[7] By 1906 the figure was 630 and rising. Keighley and Leeds, for a variety of reasons, were never quite as successful but often had 120 or so members in the early twentieth century and the Leeds ILP/Labour Party won the parliamentary seat for James O'Grady by 1906. Despite these modest numbers, which did not incorporate all socialists in the West Riding textile district, the ILP and the socialist cultural organisations, kept its support together which maintained the challenge to the Liberal Party and provided the base with a continued appeal to trade union support.

What shaped the community of the textile district of the West Riding into an in-creasingly radical and socialist region? Why did the radical traditions in West York-shire become increasingly focused upon political independence and the municipal so-cialism of the ILP?

a) Chartist, Secularist and Socialist Connections

There is no doubt that there had been many expressions of independence in this community in the half century before the ILP emerged. The factory movement, agita-tion against the New Poor Law, Chartism, the co-operative movement, religious non-conformity and trade unions, were all part of the radical traditions which emerged in West Yorkshire. Yet one should not expect that the baton was handed on from one movement to another. It has been argued that Chartism owed much to eighteenth-cen-tury radicalism and was not necessarily the forerunner of socialism. Thompson noted this in his 'Homage to Tom Maguire' (pp. 281-2) when referring to a gathering of

---

7   David Clark, *Colne Valley: Radicalism to Socialism* (London, 1981), p. 110.

Halifax veterans in 1885 in a temperance hotel with George Webber, an old physical force Chartist, toasting Mr Gladstone for his reforms. Benjamin Wilson, in his *The Struggles of an Old Chartist* (Halifax, 1887), suggested (p.40) that, 'The majority of those attending the meeting...have become men of business and in some cases employers of labour.'

A few years later local activist Fred Pickles (whose 1885-1907 letters and papers are in the People's History Museum in Manchester), raised the issue of socialism with Thomas Cooper (1804-1892), the old Leicester Chartist who was briefly living in Bradford in the late 1880s. Cooper suggested that instead of wasting his time with such socialist schemes, 'young man ...you should find something worthwhile in life rather than waste your life on impractical schemes'.

The fact is that many of the old Chartists in the West Riding did not find a home in socialist organisations such as the ILP. George White, a prominent Bradford Chartist died alone in a Sheffield workhouse in 1868, Isaac Jefferson, Bradford's Wat Tyler, was active in radical meetings in the 1860s and his son, Cornelius, joined the Bradford Political Union in 1865. The link between Chartism and the ILP was tenuous to say the least. The same goes for secularism.

The Bradford Secularist, J W Gott, who had helped to form the British Secularist League and became editor of *Truth Seeker*, was a revolutionary socialist but few of his Bradford supporters were active in the emerging Bradford ILP. One of the few prominent ones who participated was F Gazeley who became an active member of the ILP's East Ward Club in Bradford. James Bartley, a typographer and a Republican who set up a journal called *Demos* for a brief time in the late 1880s, and C Leonard Robinson, were among the few republican socialists who emerged in Bradford. Bartley recalled that:

> In 1872, however, there was not much socialism in Bradford. I remember a few young forward spirits who met occasionally, in an informal way, in "The Black Bull', an old hostelry situated close to the top if Ivegate...One of their number was a disciple of Louis Blanc [who lectured in Bradford in 1860] ....This gentleman made a proposal that a Socialist Society should be formed, but nothing came of it. This was the first suggestion to organise Socialism in Bradford of which I have knowledge.

Leonard Robinson, however, went back further and had imbibed Chartist principles as a boy and was an admirer of Ernest Jones, and a founder of a Republican club in 1870. The general tenor of this cuts across the views expressed in Eugenio F Biagini and Alastair J Reid (eds) in *Currents of radicalism: Popular radicalism, organised labour and party politics in Britain 1850-1914* (Cambridge, 1991). Their main argument is that there was substantial continuity in popular radicalism throughout the nineteenth and twentieth centuries.

Instead of Chartism and secularism, the real impetus for socialism in Bradford, and Leeds, seems to have been a lecture by William Morris, given on behalf of the quasi-Marxist Social Democratic Federation on 25 February 1884. Morris lectured in St George's Hall to an adoring crowd though he did not like the pie and pea supper atmosphere of the occasion. He later wrote to a friend stating that:

> *The Bradford lecture went off very well: a full house and all that but they are a sad set of Philistines there, and it will be a long time before we do anything with them: you see the workmen are pretty comfortable there because all the spinning and weaving is done by women and children: the latter go to the mill at 10 years old for five hours a day as half-timers: I don't think all my vigorous words (of a nature that you may well imagine) shook the conviction of my entertainers that this was the way to make an Earthly Paradise.*[8]

In fact he was wrong because Fred Jowett, George Minty and many others were there and, following Morris's formation of the Socialist League, they formed a Bradford branch in 1885 which joined with the Leeds branch. There is a surviving picture of them – about 20 or so between them – meeting to undertake propaganda and to go on to walks. Both organisations became active in organising the unorganised, unskilled and semi-skilled workers into trade unions – in the so-called new unionist phase – in the late 1880s and early 1890s. Their activities are presented by Thompson in 'Homage to Tom Maguire', through Maguire, John Lincoln Mahon, Tom Paylor, Alf Mattison, and others, who supported the demand for the eight-hour day, wrote poems and articles for *Commonweal*, the organ of the Socialist League. They were active in organising a gasworkers' strike in Leeds (Mattison, a young engineer, was secretary), in June-July 1890, the tailoresses' strike, in Leeds led by Isabella O Ford. In other words, the socialist activity in Bradford, Leeds, Halifax and other parts of the West Riding, created the basis of radical and socialist politics. But that was not sufficient alone. The socialist activity was probably greatest in Leeds, but that, as Thompson suggested, was a case of arrested development probably because of the continued domination of the Liberal trade unionists on the trades council who contained the ILP until the late 1890s, whereas in Bradford the socialist trade unionists had control of the Bradford trades council from the early 1890s. Socialism by itself was not sufficient.[9]

---

8 Philip Henderson (ed.), *The Letters of William Morris to his Family and Friends* (London, 1950), letter dated 25 February 1884.
9 Thompson, 'Maguire', p. 303.

b) Religious Influence

Religious influence was also present, if not sufficient. Admittedly the salvation of the individual soul was probably more important that the 'creation of the kingdom of heaven upon earth' but there was a religious link with the emergent ILP, although the precise relationship is under question. Tony Jowitt has argued that religious influence, and particularly Congregationalism, underpinned many of the social activities of the ILP.[10] On the other hand Leonard Smith has argued that the link was incidental and dependent upon the influence of prominent individuals, largely from the Congregationalists, Unitarians and the Church of England.[11] Although I would veer to Tony Jowitt's view more than Len Smith's, it is clear that the link was patchy and subject to change. Nevertheless, some elements of radical nonconformity were moving to the independent Labour movement.

A tenuous link was forged between religion and the Labour movement when in 1885 the Rev Dr K C Anderson, the new pastor at Horton Lane Congregational Church, shocked his congregation, which included some of the wealthiest citizens of Bradford, when he stated that 'the socialist indictment against modern society is a true bill; we cannot answer the charge'. For eight years Anderson pressed his message home to his congregation and attempted to help settle the Manningham Mills dispute. He passed his message on to T Rhondda Williams, pastor of Greenfield Congregational Chapel. It was Williams who helped form the Social Reform Union in Bradford in 1893 – which brought together about 100 of Bradford's leading figures – including Rev R Roberts, the Congregationalist minister of Frizinghall Chapel, into an organisation who surveyed unemployment and poverty in Bradford in 1894 in league with the ILP.[12] Rhondda Williams was a friend of the Rev R J Campbell, the advocate of the 'New Theology', well before Campbell formed his League of Progressive Religion and Social Thought. Williams maintained that,

> *The truth is that any minister who refuses the advocacy of social reform and confines himself to the work of individual salvation is shirking the crucial problems of modern life.*[13]

Congregationalism carried weight and influence in other areas as well, the Reverend Bryan Dale indeed being involved in the formation of a local Fabian branch in

---

10 Tony Jowitt, 'Religion and the Independent Labour Party', in Keith Laybourn and David James, *'The Rising Sun of Socialism': The Independent Labour Party in the Textile District of the West Riding of Yorkshire between 1890-1914* (Bradford, 1991), pp. 121-34.
11 Leonard Smith, *The ILP and the Churches* (Halifax, 1993).
12 Bradford Unemployed Emergency Committee, *Report*, Bradford, 1894.
13 T. Rhondda Williams, *Memoirs of T. Rhondda Williams: From Orthodoxy to Modernism*, a collection of cuttings from the *Bradford Daily Telegraph and Argus*, which does not appear to have been published as a book. A copy can be found in Bradford Local Studies Library. Keith Laybourn, 'One of the Little Breezes Blowing Across Bradford': The Bradford Independent Labour Party and Trade Unionism c. 1890-1894', in Keith Laybourn and David James in *'The Rising Sun of Socialism': The Independent Labour Party in the Textile District of the West Riding of Yorkshire between 1890-1914* (Bradford, 1991), pp. 7-8.

Halifax, along with John Lister, although he seems to have lost support within the Congregational Union as a result.

There was an analogous movement by Anglicans such as the Rev W B Graham who was active in Bradford socialism and a founder member of the Church Socialist League. He was later active in Colne Valley and helped Victor Grayson to his 1907 parliamentary by-election. Graham, who was 6ft 5 inches tall, "described himself as 6ft the socialist and 5 inches the parson". He wrote in the *Forward* (25 November 1905) that 'To me, as many others, Socialism seems a logical outcome of our Lord's teaching as applied to the modern democratic state.' There was also substantial support and sympathy from other Anglicans such as Father Bull and the priests at the House of the Resurrection at Mirfield, just outside Huddersfield, who gathered along with 200 Anglican ministers to send a signed letter of congratulations to the Labour Party/LRC on the 29 seats it won at the 1906 general election.

In addition, many leading figures of the local Labour movement were Congregationalist or Unitarians. W H Drew, who led the Manningham Mills strike, was a Congregationalist as was Fred Jowett MP, who attended the Horton Lane Congregational Chapel. Yet they carried little influence with the Yorkshire Congregational Union, the Rev Bryan Dale and Rhondda Williams also being shunned by them. Many Congregationalists such as James Hill, who was an important big businessman in Bradford, were opposed to the ILP, and Walter Sugden and W P Byles, owner of the *Bradford Observer*, were more interested in forming a new progressive alliance between the Labour and Liberal parties.

Yet religion did inspire many Labour activists to attempt to improve their local environment. They might live the life of a socialist but many, like Jowett, were driven to work for municipal socialism. Jowett wrote *The Socialist and the City* (London, 1907), an ILP pamphlet in which he argued that the future must grow from the present and that the purpose was to bring municipal institutions into harmony with the social gospel. Also reflecting this radical emphasis of the ILP, D B Foster, a Leeds ILPer, felt that after his conversion to socialism Bunyan's 'City of God' was a possibility. Once elected to Leeds City Council 'The Town Hall became to me the house of God. The city became to me the household of God.' [14]

c) Wealthy Supporters

Socialist activists and religious support provided a contest for the ILP's growth but were not sufficient in themselves. What then of the obvious influence of the many wealthy supporters which the local ILP gathered around it? There is surviving an undertaking in 1895 at which prominent individuals undertook to underwrite the costs

---

14 D. B. Foster, *Socialism and The Christ: my two great discoveries in a long search for Truth* (Leeds, 1921).pp. 27
    and 59

of the ILP in the 1895 general election with the Halifax Joint Stock bank. It was organised by John Lister, the first treasurer of the ILP, who was the owner of Shibden Hall in Halifax, a wealthy landowner, a close friend of Edward Carpenter, a Liberal who joined Labour, and an Anglican who became a Catholic. He provided the local ILP with substantial sums of money which he discounted over the years. He was its great benefactor and Keir Hardie wrote in *Labour Leader*, 'That all the gangral elements of the Labour movement descended upon Shibden Hall, much to the disgust of the Butler.'

Others in that group include France Littlewood, a woollen manufacturer/merchant from Colne Valley, and also Arthur Priestman, a Quaker, who with his brother, H B Priestman, ran one of the largest textile manufacturing businesses in Bradford. In 1906, when Fred Jowett was returned for Labour in Bradford West, Arthur became Labour leader in Bradford at the same time that his brother was the Liberal leader. On his death in 1918 his Liberal obituary writers could not work out why he supported Labour except for his genuine concern for humanity. In the case of John Lister he was concerned about the environment and had been influenced by William Morris's lectures whilst at Oxford.

d) Cultural and Social Factors

James Hinton, among other historians, has played down the importance of cultural and social factors in the evolution of the early Labour movement – seeing them as a small niche in its development. This view was challenged by Fred Reid in his various writings on socialist Sunday schools and the Labour Church movement, as did Edward Thompson in his book on *William Morris*. In the late 1970s and early 1980s Stephen Yeo felt the need to attach 'The Religion of Socialism' (*History Workshop*, 1977) with the emergence of William Morris as a socialist in 1883 and his death in 1896. He was attacked because of his views that the development of election machines in municipal elections in the mid 1890s killed off the commitment to living the life of a socialist. He was attacked, with some justice, for suggesting that the living of the life of a socialist declined rapidly in the 1890s. It was pointed out that whilst Labour churches disappeared quickly that socialist Sunday schools, ILP clubs and the Clarion movement continued to prosper until the Great War. Yeo defended himself in an article in the early 1980s entitled 'Towards making more of a moment than spirit'.[15] This statement, written by Keir Hardie in the *Labour Leader* of 15 October 1898, shows that Hardie was asking the ILPers to be practical and to organise and win elections rather than just to rely upon living the life of a socialist. To Yeo this was evidence of the process of moving away from the spirit of socialism to the pragmatism of municipal and parliamentary politics.

---

15   J A Jowitt and R K S Taylor (eds), *Bradford 1890-1914:The Cradle of the ILP* (Leeds, U. of Leeds, Adult & Education & Extramural Studies, Bradford Occasional Papers, No.2, 1980).

In the textile district of Yorkshire it is clear that the cultural side of the movement, and the religion of socialism, survived quite healthily beyond the mid-1890s. The Labour churches emerged in Bradford, Leeds, Keighley and other centres in the early 1890s offering their Sunday morning lectures and rather eclectic meetings later in the day. The movement soon declined, John Trevor its founder soon departed and *The Labour Prophet*, its organ, began to decline by the turn of the century. The Leeds and Bradford Labour churches were forced to unite at the turn of the century. However, the socialist Sunday schools which had first emerged in the early 1890s, did not begin until 1895.

Socialist Sunday Schools, originally established in Battersea, and then in Glasgow, often grew as a result of the Labour churches, although they were independent of that movement and long survived it. Indeed, there were five regional unions by 1909, in Glasgow, Edinburgh, London, Lancashire and Cheshire and Yorkshire and in 1913 Tyneside was added.

The textile district of the West Riding was well organised. *Young Socialist* in 1916 indicated schools in Bradford (Central, East Bowling, East, Great Horton, Heaton and Manningham – West Bowling seems to have gone), one at Brighouse and Halfax, three in Huddersfield at Central, Lockwood and Paddock, Kirkheaton had one, Leeds had four (Central, East, North West, South, West) and there was Wakefield developed from other Nonconformist groups with their own Sunday schools. This led to the development of the Socialist Ten Commandments and the Socialist Precepts, which were a summary of what Labour socialists stood for, particularly focussing upon respect for all men and eschewing the idea of bowing down to any man.

ILP/Labour Union/ Socialist clubs expanded rapidly throughout the 1890s and the Edwardian years. There is something of a local debate here though. David Clark wrote a book on the early history of the Colne Valley Labour constituency in 1981.[16] He argued that it was club life and the social aspect of Labour's activities, not trade unionism, that kept the Labour movement going in Colne until the enormous success of Victor Grayson in 1907 pushed the movement forward. I agree with him but suggest that whilst trade unionism was weak there, everyone who was a socialist and could be a trade unionist was so (such as George Garside). I might also add that it was the ILP which took over the radical agenda. David James in his book on Keighley Labour said much the same, although I would make the same observation. Even in Bradford, the 19 clubs and 2,000 members, of the early 1890s, although they were later reduced in number, provided the base for Labour success. They engendered a spirit of unity in the movement and worked closely together and competed with each other, for instance, in the annual cricket contest for the Fattorini Shield. By the Great War, the ILP had its own cinema in Morley Street, Bradford. There was a powerful

---

16 Clark, *Colne Valley: Radicalism to Socialism.*

club movement in Halifax, which also had its own socialist cafe. In Colne Valley, after the parliamentary by-election success of Grayson in 1907, every village had its own socialist club.

The Clarion movement, formed by Robert Blatchford in Manchester in 1891, was well established in Bradford, Halifax and Keighley. Montague Blatchford, 'Mont Blong', was active in promoting its development in Halifax, and Philip Snowden did much for its activities in Keighley. It was powerfully present in Bradford and Colne Valley. It promoted fellowship and brotherhood through the Clarion glee clubs, the Clarion Van movement, the Clarion Scouts and the Clarion cyclists. Snowden in his *Autobiography*, (London, 1934), was later to famously recall the cycling and propaganda trips where cyclists would stop off near fields and attach posters onto the backsides of cows proclaiming socialism as the hope of the world.

Yet in the end what gave the West Yorkshire labour movement its political success was the growing anti-Liberalism and its ability to tap into trade union support through policies such as the eight-hour day, 6d per hour, 48-hour week and the other demands of the unions. It is these policies which attracted the mass support which projected the ILP and Labour Party forward.

e) Anti-Liberalism

The reason for this was the wider range of discontent that was developing in the late nineteenth century textile community of the West Riding. There was certainly an anti-Liberalism developing as well as a small, but frustrated, trade union movement. Anti-Liberalism was becoming increasingly evident as the Liberal Party in West Yorkshire, dominated by the likes of Alfred Illingworth and the relatively intransigent right-wing millocracy who refused to acknowledge the radical issues of removing half-time pupils from the system, failed to acknowledge the need for new measures to deal with the unemployed or to tackle the issue of school meals to deal with poverty.

In the textile district of the West Riding the Liberals normally won 19 of the 23 seats from the mid-1880s onwards. They normally dominated the town councils of Bradford, Halifax, Huddersfield, Keighley and Leeds and normally dominated the school boards and the board of guardians. Liberal organisations were so powerful locally that they were disdainful of the working class. In Bradford they rejected the attempt by the Bradford Trades Council to put forward their secretary/president Samuel Shaftoe, a good Liberal, to stand for the municipal seat of West Bowling in Bradford. He was put forward on several occasions, and turned down in 1888, the year that the TUC annual meeting was held in Bradford, in favour of an unfair employer, one who did not pay trade union wages – Martin Field, a printer. Shaftoe described himself 'as the most kicked about football in Bradford politics.' Yet whilst he remained faithful to the Liberal Party, many of his supporters did not. Elsewhere, France Littlewood, a small merchant who later became a treasurer to the ILP, became frustrated with the Liberals who brought in Sir James Kitson to contest Colne Valley without a proper selection process – he had previously secured a seat for Herbert Gladstone in Leeds and this was seen as his reward.[17] Such Liberal attitudes mean that when the Bradford Labour Union/ILP was formed in May 1891 Alfred Illingworth, the Bradford manufacturer and MP, suggested that, 'This was merely one of those breezes which occasionally crosses Bradford.'

There was also the case of William Pollard Byles. Owner and sometime editor of the *Bradford Observer*, he was a radical Liberal who supported the case of the workers at Manningham Mills in 1890-1, fought with the support of Shipley Trades Council and against the owners of Saltaire Mills to secure the Liberal candidature for Shipley in 1892, which he lost as a result of Liberal collusion with the Unionist candidate in the 1895 general election. In 1896 he failed to become the compromise Liberal Radical candidate in the parliamentary by-election for Bradford East and eventually left Bradford politics to seek his fortunes in the more conducive political air of Manchester in 1903. The *Bradford Daily Telegraph*, a right-wing Liberal paper owned by Alfred Illingworth and his friends, included an obituary for his departure:

> *He has affluence, he has leisure, and he has ambition. That other desideratum troops of friends' is denied him, or at least if he has troops his enemies are in battalions. Owing to untoward circumstances, Mr Byles's career was so circumscribed here in Bradford that it became intolerable. To find greater space, and ampler air, he had at the age of 64 to expatriate himself, to leave all his friends and associations behind to live in Manchester. It is a hard fate but it is necessary if Mr. Byles should fulfil the political role to which he is irresistibly drawn.[18]*

Then the real abuse begins with the suggestion that you could not be in a room with him for five minutes without him disagreeing with you, that 'Dame Nature' should be blamed for his unfortunate manner. Finally it concluded that his wife was very nice and agreeable.

The final straw and perhaps the parting of the ways for many Liberals, radicals, independent Labour supporters and socialists was the parliamentary by-election in Bradford in November 1896. This came at a time when independent Labour was facing its worst years. It had done badly in the 1895 general election – described as the most expensive funeral since that of Napoleon – when it lost its only MP in Keir Hardie in West Ham South. There was discussion of a possible union of socialist forces at this time, which Hardie opposed. And then an opportunity for a radical alliance emerged in Bradford. Normally the three parliamentary seats in Bradford were won

---

17 Clark, *Colne Valley: Radicalism to Socialism.*
18 *Bradford Daily Telegraph*, 31 March 1903.

by Liberals but in the 1895 general election the Conservatives won all three and sent the Liberals 'to the bottom of the deep blue sea' returning Ernest Flower, Byron Reed and the Marquis of Lorne (the Liberals having previously described them as 'A broken Reed, a wilting Flower and a Marquis of Forlorne'). Byron Reed died and left the Bradford East seat vacant. For a time it looked as though Hardie would be the only progressive candidate to face the Tory candidate. However, at the last minute, Alfred Illingworth found a Liberal candidate, thus breaking the possibility of Hardie effectively being the sole radical candidate and picking up Liberal votes. He brought in Alfred Billson and there was a cartoon in *The Clarion* which depicted Billson being dragged from Forster Street Railway station by the scruff of his neck. The *Clarion* commented wryly that:

> *The two most important events of the week are the discovery of a sea serpent off Lowestoft and the discovery of a Liberal candidate for Bradford. They are both said to be remarkably fine specimens – the serpent being quite three hundred yards, or feet, long, and about as big round as an elephant. The Liberal candidate is not so large round as that, though quite big enough for the Emergency. He was landed also, after some trouble, whereas the other curiosity escaped.*[19]

In the wake of the contest the *Daily Chronicle* stated, appositely, that Liberalism in Bradford had been doomed to failure because for years it took no account of Labour. The people of Bradford were expected to return to Parliament, and to take their political orders from them. Illingworthism is a gospel without sympathy, comradeship, or hope for the Bradford worker, and an attempt to identify it with Liberalism has had its consequence in Keir Hardieism.[20]

f) Trade Unionism

Although a growing sense of anti-Liberalism, and the end of an old radical alliance, was, obviously, not exclusively associated with trade unionism there was a sense in which the unions were the ones who took greatest umbrage at the actions of the Liberal Party. The Bradford Society of Typographers, which represented the best paid craftsmen in the town, many of whom were Conservative or Liberal, were upset at the Martin Field affair, already mentioned, and moved towards support for an independent Labour movement when they were faced with the threat of the Thorne composing machine being introduced and with the conflict at Manningham Mills in 1890/1. The Silk Spinners' Union in Halifax was upset when its independent labour representatives – James Beever (an old Liberal) and James Tattersall were victimised by the firm of Clayton, Murgatroyd and Co. This action immediately galvanised the independent political Labour movement in Halifax.

---

19 *The Clarion*, 7 November 1896.
20 Quoted in the *Labour Leader*, 21 November 1896.

The fact is that the speeding up of textile machinery in the late nineteenth century, combing machinery being speeded up 30 per cent or more and the weavers working three looms between two weavers rather than two, plus new machinery, and increasing industrial conflict began to detach working-class support from the Liberal Party towards the new independent Labour movement that was emerging. There had been a major textile conflict in Huddersfield and area in 1884 but the Manningham Mills strike brought together the regional and local tensions in textile and trade unionism as never before. There is much written on it but briefly Samuel Cunliffe Lister, faced with the loss of his American markets due to the McKinley Tariffs, imposed wage cuts of 17 to 33 per cent upon his workforce. Eventually, between December 1890 and April 1891, 5,000 workers were locked out or struck, their strike meetings interfered with and troops were called out to maintain order and the Riot Act was read. The dispute brought together trade unionists of all persuasions and occurred at a time when trade union membership nationally and locally was expanding rapidly (3,500 in Bradford in 1886 to about 13,500 in 1893). This was perceived to be naked class warfare.[21] *The Labour Journal*, 7 October 1892, wrote that 'In the Lister strike, the people of Bradford saw plainly, as they had never seen before, that whether their rulers are Liberal or Tory they are capitalists first and politicians afterwards.'

The Bradford Labour Union, which became the Bradford ILP, was conceived in the frustrations of working men affected by the Manningham dispute. Charlie Glyde said, 'We have had two parties in the past, the can'ts and the won'ts, and it is now time we had a party that will.'[22] The Bradford Labour Union was formed in May 1891. Very quickly, it captured the support of the Bradford Trades and Labour Council (BDTC) for Ben Tillett's candidature of Bradford West against Alfred Illingworth in 1892. In 1900 the Bradford Trades and Labour Council and the Bradford ILP were united in election policies through the Municipal Election Committee and from 1902-1916 through the Workers' Municipal Federation (WMF). Although a formal member of the first arrangement the ILP did not affiliate with the WMF, although most of the BTC representatives were members of the ILP and from 1905 onwards the WMF did the election work for both WMF and ILP candidates. Halifax also developed a similar arrangement. In essence this allowed for a broader electoral policy to encompass all shades of trade union opinion with the ILP/Labour cause.

One might reflect briefly upon other factors at play in creating the Independent Labour Party and the early political Labour movement in Yorkshire.

---

21 Keith Laybourn, 'The Manningham Mills Strike, December 1890 to April 1891', in David James, Tony Jowitt and Keith Laybourn, *The Centennial History of the Independent Labour Party* (Halifax, 1992), pp.117-36.
22 *Bradford Observer Budget*, April 1891.

g) Women

Jill Liddington, in her book *Rebel Girls,* has stressed how the Women's Social and Political Union carried significant support within the West Yorkshire Labour and socialist community. Over 500 ILP women signed the *Manifesto to the Women's Social and Political Union* published at New Year 1907.

Of these 136 came from the West Riding of Yorkshire and another 146 from Lancashire. And of the fifty-eight of Emmeline Pankhurst's Women and Social and Political Union branches sprung up across the country in the first, almost a quarter lay in Yorkshire – mainly within the West Riding towns. For such Pennine textile communities in northern England were *the* heartland of early WSPU support Their very names – Halifax and Hebden Bridge, Bradford and Keighley, Leeds and Dewsbury – conjured up countless bales of wool, the racket of looms, the whirr of sewing machines'.

h) Socialist Unity

One might also reflect that the strength of the ILP in the West Yorkshire textile community meant that even at its weakest the socialist unity campaign of the mid-1890s never really took off – the Bradford ILP with more than 1,000 members in 1897 and 1898 not wanting to join with the 23 members of the SDF at that time. The later attempt to form the British Socialist Party, pressed forward by Victor Grayson from 1911 onwards, captured some general support in the textile district of the West Riding, and most obviously the ILP in Colne Valley Labour League (formed in 1899). But the CVLL never paid its dues and drifted out of the BSP, which affiliated to the Labour Party in 1916. It is clear that it was the ethical and radical issues which appealed to those who supported Labour in the textile district of the West Riding. Perhaps it was the sense of community which blocked the broader socialist approach.

Conclusion

The development of the independent Labour movement, the ILP, in the textile district of the West Riding drew upon many factors to create the interlinking and overlapping community spirit which shaped it into a heartland for Labour's growth before the Great War. There may have been old radical sentiments at play, there was clearly religious influences, cultural forces, anti-Liberalism, socialist activists acting as a core and other factors. Nevertheless, it was trade unionism, accreting to a core of hard-line socialist support, which appears to have created the successful independent Labour movement in the area, driven by the indifference and intransigence of right-wing Liberalism – Illingworthism and its kind – which was increasingly out of step with the new radicalism that was emerging.

I would, therefore, like to finish with two quotes. One is from the Bradford ILP paper *Forward* (13 January 1906) which, following Fred Jowett's parliamentary victory in Bradford West against a Conservative candidate and the Liberal nominee W Claridge, published a poem which was a sharp reminder of Liberal neglect and Labour advance.

> *A plausible weaver named Claridge*
> *Once sought for West Bradford in marriage,*
> *But was left in the lurch,*
> *She would not go to Church,*
> *In Alfred Illingworth's carriage.*

And finally, Jowett, returned as MP in 1906, wrote his memories in *What made me a Socialist* (Glasgow, 1941). Reflecting upon his early socialist meetings he wrote (p. 10)

> *These meetings were occasions for drawing together the two small groups of Socialists in Leeds and Bradford, where branches of the old Socialist League had been formed. There were less than a dozen members in the Bradford branch, and I became one of them. Although weak in numbers, we were strong in faith.*
>
> *Sometime in the summer time, the joint forces of Leeds and Bradford Socialism tramped together to spread the gospel by printed and spoken word in neighbouring villages. And at eventide, on the way home, as we walked in country lane or on river bank, we sang*
>
> *"What is this, the sound and rumour? What is this that all men hear. Like the wind in hollow valleys when the storm is drawing near. Like the rolling on of the ocean in the eventide of fear? 'Tis the people marching on".*
>
> *And we believed they were.*

The ILP in the West Riding of Yorkshire was becoming the new radicalism of the late nineteenth century driven by socialist ideas which provided the platform for the Labour Party's commitment to socialism in its 1918 Constitution. It was driven on, however, more by a sense of radical community politics than state socialism that the Labour Party committed itself to in 1918.

Liverpool Labour

John Belchem

Seemingly at odds with its current political alignment and reputation, Liverpool was by no means to the fore in the forward march of Labour. Liverpool, indeed, remained a Tory stronghold into the second half of the 20th century: the Labour Party failed to capture control of the City Council until 1955, a generation later than other urban conurbations. In the industrial north but not of it, the great seaport of Liverpool with its vast waterfront casual labour market presented a difficult challenge for the early labour movement. Casual labourers lacked the guaranteed time, relevant experience or financial resources for regular union involvement and subscription. When trade unions were eventually implanted, they were dominated by full-time officials, a bureaucratic framework soon to provoke a rank and file 'militant' reaction. As officials sought union incorporation in national agreements with employers, to which end they were prepared both to discipline and decasualise the membership, they offended against the independence and pride of the Liverpool labourer. For all its ills, casualism was a cherished symbol of independence, the best guarantee of freedom from irksome work discipline, from the tyranny of the factory bell. Syndicalist advocates of direct action found a point of entry, most notably in the city's general strike of 1911,[1] but the frequent incidence of subsequent rank and file militancy seems to have been determined less by theory and praxis than by specific grievances and traditional attitudes. Liverpool workers continued to protest against impositions and innovations – national agreements, bureaucratic structures and new work practices – which denied their residual independence and democratic local autonomy. This assertive local pride was to persist long after the decline of the docks, shipping and casualism. In the second half of the 20th century, workers in the new industrial plants of the Merseyside Development Area gained a reputation for antipathy to factory discipline and managerial prerogatives, prompting some observers to trace a cultural continuity back to the old traditions of waterside casualism and seafaring independence, the legacy of dockers who offered themselves for employment when they wished and of seamen who were able to pick and choose their ships.[2]

Alongside militant defence of workplace autonomy and independence, Liverpool workers displayed another aspect of distinctive local culture in their political affiliation. To the despair of socialists, ethno-religious sectarianism remained the principal factor in political allegiance in this port of entry, the most Celtic of English cities. Studies of sectarianism have tended to focus on violent clashes between Orange and Green without according sufficient attention to the positive benefits of confessional

1 Bob Holton, 'Syndicalism and Labour on Merseyside, 1906-1914' in H R Hikins (ed) *Building the Union: studies on the growth of the workers' movement*, Merseyside, 1756-1967 (Liverpool, 1973), pp.121-50.
2 R Bean and P Stoney, 'Strikes on Merseyside: a regional analysis', *Industrial Relations Journal*, 17 (1986), pp.9-23.

allegiance.[3]   Although restricted to those of the faith, sectarian formations were otherwise inclusive in their collective mutuality, reaching beyond the skill and gender boundaries of labour organisation. Notorious for his role in inflaming sectarian violence in the early 20th century, George Wise sustained his popularity among Protestant workers through his tontine society which offered sickness, unemployment and death insurance, and by provision of a range of leisure and recreational facilities, including the George Wise Cycling Club, the largest in the city.[4] Labour failed to make significant advance among Protestant workers, whose 'marginal privilege' was underwritten by the Tories. Committed to civic progressivism and social reform (even 'municipal socialism'), Toryism in Liverpool had a distinctive inflexion and style with the Working Men's Conservative Association at the hub of its interlocking associational network. The President of the Liverpool Carters Union, an all but exclusively Protestant occupation, was John Houlding, brewer and hotel proprietor, Orangeman, Freemason, chair of the Everton Conservative Association, city councillor, Lord Mayor (1897-98), and a key figure in founding Everton F C and in leading the breakaway group to establish Liverpool F C.[5] Local notables like Houlding continued to monopolise political positions in 'Tory town' Liverpool – there was no working-class Conservative councillor before 1914 – but as need arose, they were able to mingle at ease within the network, displaying the common touch which soon became a distinguishing (and essential) characteristic of local Tory leadership, a style perfected in Archibald Salvidge's electoral machine, perhaps the most remarkable example of British 'boss politics'. Immune to the blandishments of Westminster, 'Salvidge of Liverpool', declined the invitation to transfer to the capital to bring the national organisation of the Conservative Party up to Merseyside standards.[6] Recognising the continuing popular appeal of protectionism, Salvidge defied local 'business conservatism' to uphold Tariff Reform, championing local working-class interests against the 'lower middle-class fraud, called Liberalism or "Free Trade"'. A compound of populism, protectionism and Protestantism, Tory political hegemony in Liverpool, described by John Vincent as the deepest and most enduring Tory 'deviation' among Victorian workers, was to persist – albeit with occasional riotous fracture – well into the twentieth century, continuing to confound external critics and observers.[7] As Philip Waller noted in his magisterial study, *Democracy and Sectarianism*, it seemed 'paradoxical that the Conservatives could be so successful, without being dishonest,

3   See, for example, Frank Neal, *Sectarian Violence: The Liverpool Experience*, 1819-1914, Manchester University Press, 1988.

4   John Bohstedt, 'More than One Working Class: Protestant and Catholic Riots in Edwardian Liverpool' in John Belchem, *Popular Politics, Riot and Labour*, Liverpool University Press, 1992, pp.195-210.

5   Houlding features prominently in the vast amount of literature on football in Liverpool: see for example, D Kennedy and M Collins, 'Community Politics in Liverpool and the governance of professional football in the late nineteenth century', *Historical Journal*, 49, 3, 2006, pp.772-788.

6   Stanley Salvidge, *Salvidge of Liverpool: Behind the Political Scene, 1890-1928*, Hodder and Stoughton, 1934, chap.8.

7   J R Vincent, *Pollbooks: How Victorians Voted*, Cambridge University Press, 1967, p.61.

in Liverpool, given the grim circumstances in which much of the population lived and worked'.[8]

Confronted by the Tory narrative of British religious and constitutional freedom, the large numbers of Irish in Liverpool, technically internal migrants in a single market and United Kingdom, were reduced to the local underclass, the internal other. However, they were by no means passive victims of pervasive prejudice and denigratory stereotyping. They were soon to formulate their own versions of Irishness, an ethno-confessional affiliation which served at first protective and defensive functions against disadvantage, disability and discrimination, but then became increasingly assertive, leading to a form of Home Rule in Irish Liverpool. Soon under the control of Irish nationalist councillors, the north end of the city, indeed, was best described (in A M Sullivan's words) as 'a piece cut off from the old sod itself'.[9] Over the years, the Irish National Party (INP) was carried forward by a radicalising dynamic, driven as much by progressive change in the composition of its council members as by mounting frustration at the Liberals' failure to deliver Home Rule. On retirement from the council, members from established middle-class professions and occupations (Irish doctors, lawyers and rich businessmen) tended to be replaced by those with a more popular style, butchers, shopkeepers, penny-a-week insurance collectors, undertakers and others who attended to the daily needs of the Liverpool-Irish. Offering a form of what has been called 'Nat-Labism', a pragmatic blend of ethnic, confessional and class interests, the INP reached into parts beyond conventional 'Lib-Labism' elsewhere, seeking to ameliorate working and living conditions for the 'poor Irish'.[10] Protected by the 'Nat-Labism' of the INP, the north end was a milieu (or 'habitus') of solidarity and security, consolidated by the associational culture and collective mutuality based on the pub and the parish, inclusive cradle to grave 'welfare' extending across socio-economic and gender divisions.[11]

By the turn of the century, local-born INP councillors, second generation Liverpool-born Irish like the Harford brothers outnumbered their Irish-born counterparts, after which, some commentators suggest, the party displayed less interest in the fate of Ireland than in the immediate needs of the local Catholic community in housing and employment. This is a false distinction: the 'Nat-Labism' embraced by the younger generation of INP councillors was as ardent in commitment to Irish nationalism as to social reform, both policies exemplifying a decisive final rejection of Liberalism. Forthright in its independence from British political parties

8   For a masterly study of Liverpool Toryism, see P J Waller, *Democracy and Sectarianism: a political and social history of Liverpool 1868-1939*, Liverpool University Press, 1981.

9   *Nationalist*, 6 December, 1884.

10 The term 'Nat-Labism' was coined by Sam Davies in '"A Stormy political Career": P J Kelly and Irish Nationalist and Labour Politics in Liverpool, 1891-1936', *Transactions of the Historic Society of Lancashire and Cheshire*, 148, 1999, p.156.

11 For extensive study of the Irish National Party in Liverpool, see John Belchem, *Irish, Catholic and Scouse: The History of the Liverpool-Irish, 1800-1939*, Liverpool University Press, 2007, chaps 4 and 5.

and unequivocal in commitment to denominational education, extensive social reform and full-blown Irish nationalism, the INP under Austin Harford was the hegemonic political force in Edwardian Irish Liverpool, leaving little space or need for class, confessional or Gaelic alternatives, such as Labour Party, the Catholic Federation or Sinn Fein.

Confronted by the strength of ethno-sectarian machine politics (and the accompanying territorial skirmishes which, as in 1909, could escalate into full-scale ugly rioting), Ramsay MacDonald observed in 1910 that 'Liverpool is rotten and we had better recognize it'.[12] A year later, however, it appeared that the pattern of popular collective behaviour had been completely transformed. Encouraged by the charismatic presence of the syndicalist Tom Mann at the head of the co-ordinating strike

committee, Liverpool workers were united in unprecedented class-based industrial militancy in 1911 a direct action 'strike wave' which brought the city 'near to revolution', prompting the government to despatch a gunboat to the Mersey.[13] Seen in retrospect, the solidarity of 1911 has been imbued with mythic force, the defining inspirational point of reference for 'militant' Liverpool's radical heritage.[14] Syndicalists heralded a new era of class solidarity above the old sectarian divisions. In Dingle Ward, Fred Bower, the rolling stonemason, averred, 'they were going to put up another colour – orange on the one side, green on the other, and red down the middle'.[15] Without diminishing the subsequent inspirational force of the events of 1911, it should be noted that such class solidarity as was forged in pre-war 'radical' Liverpool is perhaps best understood in terms of the making of a 'white' working class.[16] The determination to exclude cheap 'coloured' labour brought sharply-dressed ships' stewards and catering staff, who otherwise kept themselves apart from deck hands and those who toiled in the stokeholds, into united action with Havelock Wilson's National Sailors and Firemen's Union, unaccustomed 'unity' which secured the first significant gains in the 1911 strikes. Deploying hysterical racist discourse to condemn the 'beastly' morals of the 'Chinaman', Sexton, the dockers' leader and lone Labour councillor

---

12 Quoted in Sam Davies, *Liverpool Labour: Social and Political Influences on the Development of the Labour Party in Liverpool, 1900-1939*, Keele, 1996, p.19.

13 Eric Taplin, *Near to Revolution: The Liverpool General Strike of 1911*, Liverpool, 1994.

14 Mark O'Brien, 'Liverpool 1911 and its Era: Foundational Myth or Authentic Tradition?' in John Belchem and Bryan Biggs, eds, *Liverpool: City of Radicals*, Liverpool University Press, 2011, pp.140-58.

15 'Red Riot Sunday', *Daily Post and Mercury* 26 September 1911. Bower's autobiography, *Rolling Stonemason* was republished by Merlin Press in 2015 with an introduction by Ron Noon and Sam Davies.

16 I make this point in my 'Radical Prelude: 1911' in Belchem and Biggs, *Liverpool: City of Radicals*, pp.34-5.

joined forces with INP councillors to oppose the inflow of 'alien' Asiatic labour, the 'yellow peril'.

The industrial solidarity of 1911 notwithstanding, sectarianism was by no means eradicated. As public sanction was withdrawn from the authorities and the police after 'Bloody Sunday' (when the assembled crowds on St George's Plateau supporting the striking transport workers were violently dispersed by troops and police reinforcements from Birmingham and Leeds), there was an outbreak of lawlessness, a veritable orgy of looting and old-style sectarian violence. Liverpool, in the words of the *Review of Reviews*, was rendered 'A Nightmare of Civilisation'. Ethno-sectarian cleansing continued apace – the last Catholic resident was duly forced out of the Netherfield Road. In the aftermath of the all too brief unity, Labour added six seats to that held by Sexton but advanced no further. In 1912-13, indeed, Labour lost every contest, overwhelmed by the continued popular resonance of the city's ethno-sectarian affiliations.[17]

Tom Mann addressing a crowd in Liverpool

While undoubtedly hindered by gerrymandering and other failings of the municipal electoral system itself, Labour made little advance until 1928 when it merged with the Catholic Centre Party, successor to the INP in the complex and protracted realignment of Liverpool-Irish politics following establishment of the Irish Free

---

17 Waller, *Democracy and Sectarianism*, pp.249-65

State.[18] Many of these new Labour voters, fiercely militant in defence of dockers' and other workers' independence and autonomy, still sought to banish the 'twin evils' of secularism and socialism. Policy issues were left to their leaders, the Catholic caucus, who soon gained control of the Party in alliance with authoritarian right wing trade unionists. In this Labour variant of Liverpudlian 'boss politics', critical and left-wing voices were marginalised and silenced by the authority and manipulation exercised by the Party leader, a style introduced by Luke Hogan in the 1930s and later consolidated by Jack Braddock. Chicago on the Mersey, the Braddock 'machine' which carried the party into power in 1955, was characterised as 'Cook County UK'. Dependent on unquestioning support from deprived and decaying inner city wards, the machine failed to satisfy a growing but as yet powerless left-wing base among skilled workers in outer city wards.

As the much-needed diversification of the Liverpool economy gathered pace in the 1950s and 1960s with the location of large-scale manufacturing plants alongside housing estates for former slum-dwellers in the outer areas, the pattern of politics began to change. In the absence of residential and other solidarities and with the growth of other attractions in the Merseybeat era, sectarianism steadily lost its resonance and 'class politics' became the norm[19]. Having at last attracted significant numbers of Protestant working class voters, Labour suffered a setback in the 1970s when it was blamed for failings in the urban renewal and slum clearance programme, not least when Bill Sefton, Braddock's successor, reneged on his promise not to implement the infamous Tory Housing Finance Act (1972) with its hefty rent rises. This was the point at which the Liberals under Trevor Jones ('Jones the Vote') stood forward with a brand of 'community politics' to attract support from both former Conservative and Labour voters.

By this time Liverpool had already begun its descent into seemingly irreversible economic and demographic decline. The old port economy was hit by the collapse of the colonial economic system and global restructuring, the 'triple whammy' of the end of empire, entry into the European Economic Community and containerization. The brief 'Merseybeat' period of post-war branch-plant prosperity came to a sorry end as industrial combines were apt to close their new Merseyside plants ahead of branches elsewhere once development aid and other short term advantages were exhausted. 'Merseyside militancy' served as a convenient means to justify these boardroom decisions taken far away from Liverpool, as Merseyside became known as the Bermuda triangle of British capitalism.[20] Then came the confused coalition politics of 1974-83, the 'lost decade'. In the absence of any overall party majority, the Liberals – 'in office but not in power' – controlled the city through

---

18 Davies, *Liverpool Labour*, pp.53-77.
19 K D Roberts, *Liverpool Sectarianism: The Rise and Demise*, Liverpool University Press, 2017, chap.5.
20 Merseyside Socialist Research Group, *Merseyside in Crisis*, 1980, pp.9-25.

minority and coalition administrations, hoping to enlarge their electoral base by restricting expenditure and holding down the rates. Such frugality went unacknowledged when the Conservative government introduced its controversial grant system, an ideologically-charged initiative to roll back the frontiers of the state and curb public expenditure. Having previously limited its expenditure, Liverpool considered itself unfairly treated: its targets were more stringent than those of profligate Labour authorities who had developed large base budgets during the 1970s. Furthermore, the block grant system failed to take account of the city's economic deprivation and population loss, fundamental problems which had defied solution in the absence of any coherent strategy during the 'lost decade'.[21] This was the context in which Militant quickly acquired a dominant influence within the Labour Party. Expanding beyond its initial entryist base in the Walton constituency, Militant captured the moribund party machine, reduced to an empty shell by slum clearance of the old inner-city Catholic wards. As activists gained council seats and secured support among leaders of white and blue collar public sector unions, Militant 'enforced' a decisive influence on Labour Party policy, shifting it dramatically away from its traditional right of centre position.[22]

A minority presence within the Labour council, Militant council members deployed a range of methods to get their way: secret caucusing, the 'packing' of meetings, the 'fixing' of selection procedures, the 'planting' of motions, the 'delivering' of important votes and 'intimidation', 'bully boy' tactics imported by the 'loony left' to the dismay of other Labour councillors. The media condemned the construction of an alien Leninist statelet to impose 'socialism in one city' but as recent research has shown, the Militant machine relied for the most part on the time-honoured ways and means of Liverpudlian municipal politics. Alongside ideological commitment to Leninist democratic centralism, Militant drew upon the legacy of 'boss politics' now personified by the charismatic Derek Hatton. But there were significant differences from the days of Hogan, Braddock and Sefton. There was nothing grey, remote or anonymous about Hatton's Militant machine. As a very visible 'boss' Hatton was at one with the working-class spirit of the city, the very embodiment, Jonny Ball notes, of the city's reputation: 'a bolshie, sharply-dressed, mouthy arriviste, irreverent and cocky, whingeing and wanting special treatment – the archetypal scouser'. With the articulate Hatton as front man (protected when necessary by his own 'private army'), Militant was able to reach out to the Broad Left, ordinary Labour members, elements of the old left and above all, true scousers – 'the Good Liverpool working-class stock' rather than 'petit-bourgeois' academics and incomers, the 'Sainsbury's Set' of moderate Labour Councillors resident in the salubrious suburbs of the south end of the city. Beyond the much-criticised intimidation exercised within the Party, Militant

21 Michael Parkinson, *Liverpool on the Brink: One city's struggle against Government Cuts*, Policy Journals, 1985.
22 Diane Frost and Peter North, *Militant Liverpool: A City on the Edge*, Liverpool University Press, 2013.

was buttressed by a genuine wave of popular support in 'the city that dared to fight'[23]: massive demonstrations, huge rates of participation in city-wide strikes, and opinion polls all confirmed widespread approval for the council's implacable opposition to Thatcherite policies. Militant propounded a convincing narrative in which, as Ball notes, 'all the intricacies of local government finance, the restructuring of British capitalism and the long-term decline of industry were condensed into a struggle between an overbearing Thatcher versus a subjugated, underprivileged Liverpool: "I'm not a Marxist", as one councillor said, "I don't even believe in all this political stuff. I just don't think it's fair."' In the end, there seemed no alternative to confrontation, to Militant's 'blackmail and bankruptcy' strategy.[24]

In place of the old sectarian divisions no longer relevant to the common sense of 'scouse' identity, pride and grievance, Militant looked to the working class in monolithic but distinctly old-fashioned terms. Its workerist ideology fetishised the 'authentic', blue-collar worker: the prototypical, unionised, male, white, straight, working-class scouser. There was no truck with what Hatton decried as the 'yuppie socialism' of the London left. Seemingly oblivious of the inequalities that arise in class society in terms of race, gender and sexuality, Militant dismissed the new identity politics of gay rights, racial and sexual equality as a distraction from the fundamental class struggle, along for good measure with New Age environmental and ecological movements. Even the white-collar organised workers of NALGO found themselves condemned along with feminists and black activists and other middle-class peddlers of 'fringe issues' when the union voted narrowly to reject indefinite strike action and the notorious redundancy notice strategy, the 'grotesque chaos' so vigorously condemned by Neil Kinnock at the 1985 Labour Party Conference. There were bitter conflicts in the north end of the city with those involved in the housing cooperative movement, and even worse relations with black rights groups in the south end.[25] To its discredit – and eventual cost – Militant snubbed and ignored the associational endeavours and representational needs of ethnic, gender, special interest and minority groups, formations very different in composition and character from the old sectarian allegiances.

Forced to retreat into creative accounting and financial irregularities when the strategy backfired of issuing 31,000 redundancy notices, some 49 (later 47) Labour councillors were surcharged by the District Auditor (the fines were met by donations from the public) and then discharged from office. Following an inquiry into the activities of Militant by Labour's National Executive, Derek Hatton, Tony Mulhearn and half a dozen others were expelled from the Party. An unelected Liberal-Tory junta

23 Peter Taaffe and Tony Mulhearn, *Liverpool: a city that dared to fight*, Fortress Books, 1988
24 Jonny Ball, '"Militant Liverpool" as Liverpool Exceptionalism: The Rise, Fall and Character of the City Council, 1983-1987', *Transactions of the Historic Society of Lancashire and Cheshire*, 166, 2017, pp145-86.
25 Liverpool Black Caucus, *The Racial Politics of Militant in Liverpool: The black community struggle for participation in local politics 1980-1986*, Merseyside Area Profile Group and the Runnymede Trust, 1986.

took over from the dismissed Labour administration and sought to reverse everything associated with Militant, symbolised by restoring the office of Lord Mayor and appointing Trevor Jones to the post. Their tenure proved short-lived. By-elections to replace the banned 47 councillors (only 13 of whom were members of Militant) followed by council elections in May 1987 returned the Labour Group, in somewhat more pliant form, as the majority on the Council. There followed a period of bitterness and internecine dispute as councillors identified as either 'Official Labour' or 'Liverpool Labour' drew different lessons from the torrid years of 1983-87. There was division too on the industrial front when workers for the Mersey Docks and Harbour Company refused to cross a picket line. The subsequent dispute which lasted from 1995 to 1998 drew upon the resources of Women on the Waterfront and pioneer use of the World Wide Web to secure support among dockworkers across the globe. All that was missing in this remarkable (and under-acknowledged) display of rank and file militancy was the official support of the Transport and General Workers Union, a familiar reprise in Liverpool labour history.[26] Once again the Liberal Democrats took advantage of all the division, recrimination and confusion, returning to head the Council through the years of 'new Labour' national government. However, when the Tories got back into government in coalition with the Liberal Democrats, Liverpool, never a city to conform to the national pattern, reverted to (and has remained) Labour. There was at least one positive aspect to the travails and complexities of the post-Militant era. The Conservative vote collapsed almost completely in what had once been the most Tory city in the country.

---

26 Brian Marren, 'The Liverpool Dock Strike, 1995-1998: a resurgence of solidarity in the age of globalization', *Labor History*, 57, 4, 2016, pp.463-81.

Labour and Communist Politics in the City of Oxford between the Wars

Duncan Bowie

The focus of this article is the relationship between the two parties in the period between 1918 and 1939. It forms part of a book length study of progressive politics in the city to be published in November 2018. Oxford presents an unusual case study for two main reasons – the city with its university and its industry, centred on the Cowley motor factory, allows for an analysis of the interaction

Against War and Fascism

between the university based socialist intellectuals and the local working class trade unionists; second, the Communist Party had significant influence in the local working class movement and on the Labour Party itself in two periods – the early 1920s and the late 1930s. Before considering the inter-war period, which is the main focus of this article, it is important to summarise the history of the Oxford labour movement in the pre-war period.

Progressive Politics before the First World War

While the Labour Party only became dominant within the traditional Tory city of Oxford in the mid-1960s, there had been a vigorous progressive political tradition within city politics which can be traced back to the 1830s. In the 1840s and 1850s there was a group of radical councillors on the Oxford City Council, including the Chartist James Josiah Faulkner and two radical mayors, John Towle and Isaac Grubb. Oxford had an active branch of the Reform League in the 1860s led by the university academics, James Thorold Rogers and Goldwin Smith. Oxford had a series of Liberal MPs, though some were to lose their early radicalism and between the 1880's and the First World War, Oxford was a Tory city.

The 1880s however saw a revival of radicalism in the city with the development of an 'extreme' section in the Oxford Reform Club, led by J A Partridge who had previously been involved in the Birmingham Reform League. In a lecture in November 1883 on land nationalisation, chaired by Thorold Rogers who had become

MP for Southwark, Partridge claimed that 'he was there that night to hoist the flag of social democracy in Oxford'. The university's Russell Club then hosted lectures by Henry Mayers Hyndman on 'social democracy' and by William Morris on 'Art under Plutocracy'. In March 1884, the Russell Club was addressed by the American land reformer Henry George, where George defended his proposals against an attack by the economist, Alfred Marshall. Partridge resigned from the Oxford Liberal Association and set up his own Radical Association. In December 1884, the mathematician, Charles Faulkner, a close friend of William Morris, organised meetings of advanced thinkers in the city to seek support for socialist ideas. This led to him introducing a socialist programme to a meeting of the Radical Association. This was adopted, which led to Partridge's resignation, on the basis that he was 'opposed to the principle of confiscation as applicable to the great problems of land and capital'. Faulkner then took over the leadership of the Radical Association which then became the Oxford Socialist League. The launch meeting was attended by both Morris and Edward Aveling. The Socialist League continued to hold meetings in Oxford until 1899, though from 1896, the organisation operated as the Oxford and District Socialist Union. After the turn of the century, meetings continued but appear to be confined to members of the university and chaired by 'respectable Liberals' such as the historian Professor York Powell or the Fabian political philosopher, Sidney Ball with no involvement in trade union or municipal affairs, although one member, Joseph Clayton gave a series of talks on 'the land and the parish' in villages around Oxford.

In 1888, Oxford trade unionists founded the Oxford Trades Council, the first working class based organisation in the city. It was based on the printers' union at Oxford University's Clarendon Press in Jericho, where its first president, George Hawkins was a compositor. Hawkins immediately stood as a candidate for the city council as an 'independent'. Hawkins had some support from the Liberal party but still came bottom of the poll, though in 1890, he was elected as a Liberal for West ward. Another printer, Brownjohn, stood as an independent in a subsequent by-election, also coming bottom of the poll, and from then onwards, the Trades Council, rather than standing their own candidates, sent questionnaires to the Liberal and Tory candidates focusing on council contracts specifying workers be paid at trade union rates, provision of allotments, free public library and arguing that council meetings should be held in the evening when working men could attend without loss of wages. The Trades Council tried unsuccessfully to persuade the Liberal Party to adopt working class candidates. In 1899, the Trades Council responded negatively to an approach by the ILP leader, Keir Hardie in relation to running candidates and appear to have concluded that independent labour representation in the city was not possible.

Oxford however witnessed the growth of more militant working class activity with the founding of a branch of the Social Democratic Federation in 1896. This appears to have been initiated by a group of students at Ruskin College, including the group's secretary Len Cotton. The group took their socialist propaganda onto the streets holding meetings at the Martyrs memorial in St Giles'. Speakers at meetings included Hyndman, James Connolly, Lorenzo Quelch and George Lansbury. A number of meetings were attacked by groups of students. Some meetings were closed down by the police, which led to a controversy over the right to free speech.

The turn of the century witnessed a revival of the Trades Council, which by now had strengthened its links with a group of Liberal councillors. The initiative for an independent labour representation in the city actually came from the city rector, Christian socialist and historian of medieval political theory, A J Carlyle, who in 1901, together with a group of trade unionists, led a campaign to set up a municipal housing association. The group ran Charles Broadhurst as an independent candidate for the city council for the West ward. Broadhurst won the support of the Trades Council and stood as a 'labour' candidate on a platform of working class housing, municipalisation of the trams and payment of workers on council contracts at trade union rates. He still came bottom of the poll. However, the campaign led to the establishment in January 1902 of a Municipal Labour Representation Association, led by Carlyle but with representation from the Trades Council and the University based Fabian Society led by Sidney Ball and by lecturers at Ruskin College, Bertram Wilson and Hastings Lees Smith (the latter was to become a Liberal MP in 1910, before switching to Labour in 1919 and becoming a Labour MP in 1922). The Association was formed despite the opposition of Liberal councillors who had previously collaborated with the Trades Council. The MLRA was to stand candidates in successive elections but by 1904 decided to collaborate with the Liberal Party. A tailor, Jabez Clifford, stood in East ward as a Lib-Lab candidate but was still defeated, even though a Liberal candidate was successful. An independent Labour candidate in West ward was also unsuccessful.

A group of trade unionists, led by Broadhurst and the building worker, G S Beesly, who had been an active radical in the 1870s, rejecting the Liberal alliances, decided in January 1905 to set up a branch of the Independent Labour Party. The organisation affiliated to the national Labour Representation Committee. It organised public meetings and assisted by students from Ruskin college, organised demonstrations on unemployment. It collaborated with the Trades Council and the Municipal Labour Representation Association and ran candidates in the local elections, albeit unsuccessfully. An Oxford branch of the Clarion Cycling Club was also active. In 1906 the Trades Council established an Oxford Labour Representation Committee. There was still opposition from some Liberal trade unionists and the ILP was more active in election campaigns that most trade unions in the city and there were divisions between those who wanted to stand as independents and those who were happy to collaborate with the Liberals. A new agreement between the ILP and the Trades Council in 1909 created a more united labour movement, with Labour candidates standing in all four wards. However, the Trades Council remained relatively inactive focusing its attention on supporting trade unionists in a series of industrial disputes, and labour candidacies tended to rely on the ILP. A new ward-based organisation was established by the Trades Council in early 1914.

With the declaration of war, the Trades Council announced it would not contest by-elections. The organised labour movement in Oxford appears to have taken a patriotic stance and there is no record of any protests in Oxford against the war. The ILP appears to have been silent while the British Socialist Party (successor to the SDF) wrote to the mayor of Oxford assisting to help 'mitigate all sufferings'. Protests against the war centred on the university, with a series of conscientious objectors and with the establishment of a university-based branch of the Union for Democratic Control of Foreign Policy (UDC). The Trades Council secretary was a member of the tribunal which considered cases of conscientious objection. The Trades Council was also represented on the local National Service Committee. The Trades Council rejected an invitation to join the Peace Negotiation Committee and decided not to 'to entertain peace circulars'. It even refused to discuss the issue of penal conditions on conscientious objectors and was cautious about collaborating with university based socialist groups who appeared as more radical, and a university led initiative for a joint committee was not pursued. The Trades Council focused its attention on working conditions and was also involved in a survey of local housing conditions and argued for a post-war programme of council housebuilding. Although Trades Council representatives had joined a number of civic institutions, they did not persuade the Mayor, alderman and councillors to co-opt any representatives of 'labour' to fill wartime vacancies. The consequence was that in January 1918 as the end of the war was in sight, the Trades Council re-established its sub-committee on labour representation, which invited trade unions to nominate candidates for the anticipated post-war elections. In March 1918, the moderate trade unionist, William King of the printers' union, was co-opted to fill a vacancy, though the co-option was opposed by the more socialist trade unionists. The Trades Council nominated an ILPer Harris to fill a second vacancy but this was voted down by the city council leadership.

As hostilities ended therefore, the Trades Council was under moderate leadership with its representatives embedded in a range of civic institutions including the city council. The armistice was followed immediately by a general election. The Trades Council considered standing a candidate – Cllr King declined to stand and while the trade unionist Margaret Bondfield was mentioned, it was decided not to invite a candidate who had no local connections. The Trades Council then considered a proposal to issue a manifesto calling on trade unionists not to support either Conservative or Liberal candidate, but this was not agreed. The Conservative candidate, the historian J A Marriott defeated the Liberal candidate by a substantive margin. The university had its own parliamentary seats – in fact two seats compared with the city's single seat. Labour supporters in the university nominated Sanderson-Furniss of Ruskin as their Labour candidate, who polled 335 votes, losing out to two Conservatives.

The labour movement in the city was however more organised when it came to the local elections in the following May. Fred Ludlow of the printers' union, who was secretary of the Trades Council, was returned to the city council for West ward. He was however the only one of seven candidates supported by the Trades Council and Coop not to lose his deposit. Ludlow defeated the third Tory by the narrow margin of 13 votes, the Liberals having decided not to stand candidates in the ward. He joined William King, who had been co-opted during the war. So, Labour had two councillors, compared with 21 Liberals, 25 Tories and 12 university councillors (the university having its own direct representation on the city council). The Tories also had seven aldermen to the Liberals' five. Ludlow was however unimpressed by his fellow councillors. He reported back to the Trades Council that: "The atmosphere of the Council chamber was against anything of a progressive nature. They do not like, or rather, I am afraid, they fear a proper discussion; they do not want the facts to be faced – there is no room in any building in Oxford where you could enjoy a more comfortable snooze than you could in the Council chamber."

Clash between Moderates and Militants in the early 1920s

The post-war period witnessed a revival of the pre-war socialist organisations – the Socialist Labour Party re-established a local branch in early 1919, with Keefe of the engineers' union as secretary. The group had links with Ruskin and also involved T Wigington of the postal workers' union. Keefe was also involved with a local branch of the Russian Freedom Committee, which held a meeting addressed by Sylvia Pankhurst. A group of students at Ruskin re-established the local ILP branch, which appears to have lapsed in 1914 with the outbreak of the war. Fred Smith of Ruskin was secretary; Bayliss who had been active in the ILP before the war was secretary and Fred Ludlow became president. The speakers at the inaugural meeting, John Coley and George Smith, were both Ruskin students, though Mr Goodenough of the Cooperative Union was chairman. In November 1919, a Labour Club was established at the university, following an appeal by Arthur Henderson and Sidney Webb for middle-class support.

In February 1918, the national Labour Party adopted a constitution which allowed for individual membership. However, while a constituency Labour Party was established for the North Oxfordshire parliamentary seat, centred on Banbury, in September 1919, it was not until January 1920 that the Oxford Trades Council initiated the process of establishing a local Labour Party. The initiative came from Ludlow and the inaugural conference was chaired by Horrobin of the railway clerks' union. Representatives of 16 trade union branches attended, together with representatives from the Coop, Ruskin college and the YMCA debating society. The SLP sent Wigington as a representative. The British Socialist Party was not represented. There were 18 individual members, including Rev A J Carlyle and several active members of the ILP. Dr Henry Gillett, who was to be elected as an independent councillor and was later Lord Mayor, also attended. The Liberal Alderman Carter, of Pusey House and the Christian Social Union sent his support, as did Dr Stansfield, the vicar of St Ebbes'. There was no representation from the University Labour Club. The only attendee to vote against establishing a local Labour Party was Frimbley, who had been secretary of the Trades Council before the war and was now a magistrate.

Wigington of the SLP was elected to the post of provisional chairman. The majority of the other 12 members of the executive committee were more moderate trade unionists. The committee included Fred Ludlow and Rev Carlyle, though Wigington also had the support of Hector Prickett of the carpenters. Not satisfied that the Labour Party was sufficiently socialist, Wigington sought to exert influence over the Trades Council by arguing that the Trades Council should continue with its own political activity rather than pass this role to the Labour Party. Wigington then formed an alliance with Frimbley who was opposed to the Trades Council affiliating to the Labour Party. Other trade unionists argued that the Trades Council should concentrate on supporting the trade unions rather than get involved in socialist politics. The Labourites led by Ludlow were therefore defeated by a combination of members who thought the Labour Party was insufficiently socialist and those who thought it was too socialist, with the Trades Council deciding on a vote of 21 to 12 to have nothing to do with the Labour Party. Wigington then resigned his Labour Party position and the party committee, now led by Fred Ludlow, had an emergency meeting to decide whether the Labour Party could continue without the Trades Council's support. With the Labour Party in disarray, the Trades Council decided in March 1920 to establish its own electoral committees for the four wards. It also amended its constitution to include in its objectives political as well as industrial propaganda. Wigington however failed in his attempt to become Trades Council president, losing to F Timms of the postal workers. Refusing requests from the Labour Party for financial support, the Trades Council selected its own candidates for the forthcoming local elections. Wigington tried to get the candidates to commit themselves to 'ownership and control of industry by the workers', while Prickett objected to some potential candidates 'on the possible doubt to their political convictions'. After a split vote, all five candidates nominated by individual trade unions were accepted.

Wigington and Prickett however continued with their campaign to capture the Trades Council from the moderates. The Trades Council carried a proposal from the railwaymen to convert the Trades Council into a Council of Action which would have enabled co-options from the Co-op and political organisations. The three leading moderate trade unions, the printers, carpenters and engineers, then disaffiliated from the Trades Council. The Trades Council then by a narrow majority of 22 votes to 19, supported workers ownership and control of industry, with Wigington declaring that he was 'out to smash the system'. Three of the council candidates, Frimbley, North and Surrage withdrew their candidacies as they did not agree with the new political platform. Timms was eventually forced to close the meeting because Wigington refused to stop talking. After the meeting, he also withdrew his council candidacy. The two sitting Labour councillors, King and Ludlow, announced that they would sit as Independents and not be accountable to the Trades Council. In September the Trades Council reaffirmed its position on workers control and rejected on a 24-15 vote a proposal from the printers' union that Wigington apologise for his behaviour. Timms then resigned his position as Trades Council president and said he was considering standing as an Independent Labour candidate in the council elections. The majority of the members of the four ward election committees also resigned. The Trades Council with only two candidates – Keefe in East ward and Gallop in West ward, though the latter, who was a moderate was only approved after a split vote. Both candidates were heavily defeated.

In July, a unity conference established a national Communist Party, based on the British Socialist Party but incorporating some branches of the SLP and some other smaller socialist groups. In November an Oxford branch was formed, with Hector Prickett as secretary. The Communist Party then applied to affiliate to the Trades Council only to be refused as ineligible for membership. An application from the local ILP was treated in a similar manner. The Trades Council continued to disintegrate as the railway clerks and boot and shoemakers also disaffiliated. Ludlow appealed for tolerance and an adoption of a policy all trade unions could accept. The printers also tried to persuade the Trades Council to focus on municipal propaganda rather than political propaganda. Gallop was more explicit – he wanted 'to keep out sections with purely political ends, such as communists'.

It was perhaps fortunate that increasing unemployment provided a distraction from internal faction fights. In January 1921, the Trades Council decided to revive the campaign on which the ILP had led before the war. Claiming there were now 1,500 unemployed in the city, the Trades Council led a deputation to the city council to call for a public works programme. While Ludlow and Harris, who had been active in the ILP before the war) were involved in this initiative, Wigington and Prickett were absent. The initiative had some success as the council set up communal kitchens and introduced a series of public works schemes – work on the city corporation farm, painting of the meat market and municipal buildings and works on a bridge and on the river embankment.

In March 1921, the Trades Council discussed the threatened general strike by the 'triple alliance' of miners, railwaymen and transport workers. Ludlow strongly supported the strike. Shepherd, who had been a member of the BSP and was presumably now in the Communist Party, argued that 'if the miners went down, the workers would lose all they had striven for in the last hundred years'. Wigington announced that 'capitalism was on its last legs'. A meeting of support was held in St Giles' addressed by two miners – George Williams from South Wales and Frank Mackay from Northumberland. When the strike was cancelled on 'black Friday', Ludlow called for a more united trades union movement, while Shepherd declared that 'only when class consciousness rose above personality of individuals would the success of the common cause pass from indifference, doubt, confusion, despair and difficulty to triumph'.

The divisions within the Trades Council however did not go away. While the Trades Council agreed to support King and Ludlow and an electoral policy was incorporated into its constitution, trade unions refused to contribute to the election fund or to reimburse the councillors for their work. Wigington called for the councillors to resign from council committees. Ludlow refused arguing that they had stopped the council reducing employees' wages. The Liberal-leaning *Oxford Chronicle* published some hints for Trades Council members:

1) *Don't come to meetings.*
2) *If you do come, come late.*
3) *If the weather, or the railway service doesn't suit you, don't think of coming.*
4) *If you do attend a meeting, find fault with the work of the officers and other members.*
5) *Never accept an office as it is much easier to criticise than do things.*
6) *Get sore if you are not appointed on a committee, but if you are, do not attend the meetings.*
7) *If asked by the chairman to give your opinion regarding some important matter, tell him you have nothing to say. After the meeting tell everyone how things ought to be done.*
8) *Do nothing more than is absolutely necessary, but when other members roll up their sleeves and willingly, unselfishly use their ability to help matters along, howl that the association is run by a clique.*
9) *Hold back your dues as long as possible, or don't pay at all."*

The Trades Council discussed re-establishing a local Labour Party and selecting a parliamentary candidate – Sir Sidney Olivier, Fabian and governor of Jamaica was suggested. Wigington argued against having a baronet as candidate: "The workers wanted young men to represent them – men in their twenties – not old fossils". Most unions opposed selecting a candidate. Only five of the nine unions supported re-establishing the Labour Party. The printers and other moderate trade unionists in fact were increasing sympathetic to the radical Liberal parliamentary candidate, Frank Gray, who opposed Lloyd George's coalition government and in fact the Trades Council held a special meeting to hear him. Wigington tried to stop the Trades Council meeting Gray but was voted down by 14 votes to 13. Gray also met members of individual trade unions. The Trades Council ran candidates in all four wards in the local elections, all being defeated. The candidates were mainly trade unionists, including the communists Shepherd and Prickett, but included Mrs Sanderson Furniss, wife of the principal of Ruskin, and Mrs Carter, the wife of the Liberal alderman. William King had retired from the council, leaving Ludlow as the only 'labour' member.

This failure convinced the Trades Council that a local Labour Party was necessary. Its electoral committee announced that it was now the Oxford Labour Party and invited applications from individuals as well as applying for affiliation to the national Labour Party. Ludlow was enthusiastic: "The recruitment of individual members from outside the trade unions will promote a healthy critical atmosphere .... I have reason to believe that the party may take a strong line to prevent itself from being a dumping ground for certain anti-social theories or their adherents." There was apparently no opposition within the Trades Council, with Hyde of the workers' union congratulating Wigington on his conversion to parliamentary methods. The Trades Council send delegates to the Labour Party as did the Co-op and individual trade unions. At the first AGM of the new party in April 1922, Ludlow became secretary and Fred Smith of Ruskin treasurer. Somewhat surprisingly, Wigington, who had generated such divisions two years earlier, again became chairman. The communist, Shepherd, was also on the committee. Shepherd tried to get the Trades Council committed to supporting only Labour candidates in the council elections and to picket the polling stations with 'Vote Labour' placards. This however split the Trades Council, with several members arguing that this was interfering with 'political liberties' of individual trade unionists. Shepherd's proposal was defeated. When a proposal to accept affiliation from the communist-sponsored unemployed association was not carried, with the chair using his casting vote, Shepherd and his supporters walked out.

The split within the Oxford labour movement had been reopened. The moderates argued that the Trades Council should revert to being a 'purely industrial body' while also arguing for support for Frank Gray as a 'good friend of the workers'. The woodworkers and bookbinders withdrew from the Trades Council. The postal workers decided not to nominate Wigington to the Trades Council, but he soon reappeared as a delegate from the transport workers. The postal workers then disaffiliated, saying 'they would only return when business is conducted properly'. Wigington responded that 'if they wanted a fight, let them; and it would be to their sorrow and the sorrow of Labour in Oxford, and the Right Wing would go down, right down underneath'. Given Wigington's role as Labour Party chair, a new split in the party was unavoidable. The Sanderson-Furnisses demanded a special meeting to expel Wigington. Shepherd then proposed that the Sanderson-Furnisses, Ludlow and their ally, the educationalist Mary Stocks, be expelled instead. Shepherd's proposal was defeated, but the moderates had had enough and Ludlow resigned his position as secretary. The militants also took control of North ward branch, which had been the power base of the leading moderates, with Hector Prickett in effect taking over from Mary Stocks. Fred Smith of Ruskin had also had enough of factionalism and with the party's finances in disarray, resigned as party treasurer. With the Labour Party no longer in a fit state to run an election campaign, Wigington then tried to persuade the Trades Council to fight the parliamentary election. The Trades Council chairman, Harris said this was a matter for the Labour Party. Wigington put his proposal to the vote, but was defeated by twelve votes to ten, with eight delegates abstaining. Hyde of the workers union attacked the left faction as 'pseudo Lenins and Trotskys' whose 'object was to be that of obstructing the ordinary business, harassing the chairman, dogging the secretary, and generally rendering the proceedings of the Council entirely futile'. He called for 'rank and file moderates', to unite to defeat the extremists, to save the Trades Council from degenerating 'into an instrument for the use of a section which aims at the ultimate subversion of the trade union movement.' Turning to the Oxford Labour Party, Hyde felt that that organisation "has under the chairmanship of an avowed communist, reached such a point of absurdity that no sane politician would accept nomination as its candidate and few sane electors could be found to vote for its nominee."

Harris resigned as Trades Council president. A proposal to disaffiliate from the Labour Party was only narrowly defeated and several members refused to serve as delegates to the party. Some of the Labour Party's adopted municipal candidates also stood down. Ludlow, the only Labour councillor said he would not stand as a nominee of either the Labour Party or the Trades Council. The six building trade unions however decided to support Ludlow and another candidate. The communist, Shepherd, threatened to stand himself in all four wards, attacking Ludlow for 'stampeding the workers into the Liberal ranks'. Ludlow replied that "no-one has fought harder than I have done in the cause of labour .... We can only have peace apparently if we are content to be led by the nose by Wigington and Shepherd .... He did not agree with communism if it represented anything like what they had seen in the last twelve months." He added that as a city councillor "he had put a Labour policy into practice – a Labour policy as he understood Labour ideals and policy to be." Ludlow was re-elected at the top of the poll in West ward. All the other Labour candidates, including Shepherd, were defeated. The Liberals took control of the council from the Tories. In the parliamentary election which followed, the Liberal Frank Gray defeated the sitting Tory, Marriott, becoming the first Liberal MP for the city since 1881. There was no Labour candidate.

The Trades Council continued to wrangle over the issue of whether or not to support the Labour Party. Ludlow continued to promote the party and by November 1922, the party had revived. Fred March took over Ludlow's secretarial role, with Rev Carlyle and the radiochemist Professor Soddy becoming vice-presidents. Given the party was trying to re-establish an alliance of trade unionists and progressive academics, it is perhaps surprising that at the AGM in April 1923, Wigington was elected president, defeating Ludlow by 34 votes to 11. The communist, Hector Prickett, became treasurer. The ward organisation was re-established and a womens' section formed. A delegate was sent to national conference. Shepherd was also on the executive committee. Wigington gave a talk on the history of May Day, while a week later both Wigington and Ludlow spoke at a May Day rally in St Giles. Labour candidates stood in the local elections, again unsuccessfully. When the general election was called in December 1923, there was no Labour candidate, with Frank Gray being re-elected. The first Labour government took office at Westminster.

The defeated candidate petitioned against Gray's election, and Gray was unseated for corrupt practice. The Labour Party decide to contest the by-election. Nominations for the candidacy were invited from trade unions, the Communist Party and the ILP, both being affiliated organisations. The national Labour Party agent advised the party to select 'one of

GDH Cole

the professional classes'. The choice fell on Kenneth Lindsay, a researcher for the economic historian, R H Tawney. Lindsay's main Oxford link was the fact that as a student he had founded the Oxford University Labour Club. Ludlow was opposed to the selection of a 'blackcoated man' and tried to get the Trades Council to disown the candidate, only losing the vote on the casting vote of the chairman, March, who also happened to be the Labour Party secretary. Trade unionists were divided, with many trade unionists publicly supporting the Liberal candidate, the cricketer, Christopher Fry. Ludlow however appears to have been reconciled with Lindsay as he chaired a Town Hall meeting. George Lansbury and other MPs visited Oxford to support the campaign, as did Fenner Brockway, the secretary of the ILP. The Conservative, Robert Bourne was returned, though Lindsay with 2,769 votes managed to save his deposit.

The Trades Council re-nominated Lindsay as candidate, but Lindsay decided that as he lived in London, he would contest Harrow. Ludlow was then selected, apparently without opposition, to stand in his stead. The Trades Council secretary, Penny commented that 'they must be represented by their own class'. Ludlow stated that 'whether he won or lost the election he would not run away'. Labour said he was in full agreement with the programme in

Labour's national manifesto. He supported nationalisation of the mines and railways. One of his meetings was chaired by A D Lindsay, the master of Balliol college; another by the Liberal councillor, Dr Gillett, with G D H Cole also on the platform. In the October poll, Ludlow came third with 2,260 votes, the Tory Bourne being re-elected. Labour also failed to win any seats in the council elections which followed. Gillett's support for Ludlow caused divisions within the Liberal party. Gillett refused to resign his seat though later changed his status to that of an independent. He was a prominent Quaker who was later to help found Oxfam.

The eighteen months after the general election were a period of consolidation for the Oxford Labour Party. In August 1925 a full- time agent was appointed but Labour candidates continued to be unsuccessful in municipal contests. The selection of a parliamentary candidate was considered but not pursued. The printers still wanted the Trades Council to run municipal candidates independently of the Labour Party. The Labour agent was allowed to address the Trades Council, but one delegate claimed argued that 'at least half the trade unionists in Oxford were not, nor were likely to become, members of the Labour Party'. The communists were however still influential within the Trades Council, which in March 1925 affiliated to the communist-sponsored National Minority Movement, sending two delegates to the NMM's London conference in September. The Trades Council nominated municipal candidates to the Labour Party, only to find one of its nominees, Bowles of the railwaymen, rejected on the basis of his Communist Party membership. The Trades Council supported a Communist Party appeal for funds, while delaying its payment of a £1 affiliation fee to the Labour Party and rejecting a request for a donation. The council however maintained its Labour Party affiliation, but after protests from moderate trade unionists cancelled its NMM affiliation on the basis of a 11-10 vote.

With the start of the General Strike, the Trades Council turned itself into an emergency committee, co-opting Alfred Barratt Brown, the Ruskin principal, and Trotter, the Labour Party agent. G D H Cole had been booked to speak on education but changed his topic to the coal crisis. The Trades Council published a daily strike bulletin. Cole and Trotter spoke at a rally, and a second demonstration was chaired by Trotter and addressed by Cole and Ellen Wilkinson MP. A further meeting was addressed by Oliver Baldwin, the Labour supporting son of the Prime Minister and by Lady Cynthia Mosley, who claimed that 'she had been down several mines and knew the conditions'. With the TUC General Council calling off the strike, the Trades Council demanded either a speaker from the TUC or 'an adequate written explanation'.

From the General Strike to the Popular Front

Unfortunately the unity of action in the Oxford labour movement was shortlived. The national Labour Party had determined that members of the Communist Party were ineligible for Labour Party membership, so when the Trades Council's secretary, Bowles, was nominated for the position of delegate to the annual Labour Party conference, there were objections, although the nomination was reaffirmed. Hector Prickett then argued that as communists were disqualified, the Trades Council should not make nominations for Labour Party positions. The Trades Council however decided to nominate two communists, Richardson and Loynd, only to have the nominations rejected. In April the Trades Council established a Council of Action and an Oxford Trade Union Defence committee to fight the Conservative government's Trades Disputes Bill, with the Trades Council collaborating with the Labour Party, the Co-op, Ruskin college and the University Labour Club. However, an offer to speak from Wal Hannington of the communist-sponsored National Unemployed Workers' Movement was declined and a conference of the National Minority Movement boycotted, so there were clearly divisions within the local campaign. When the Bill was passed, the committee was dissolved. The new law meant that the Trades Council had to disaffiliate from the Labour Party and delete 'political propaganda' from its objectives. The Trades Council also had to turn down any request from the Labour Party for financial or electoral assistance.

In 1928, the city boundaries were extended to include Headington and Cowley. The Labour Party branch in Headington had been active since 1924. However in the 1929 local elections all the Labour candidates in the ward, some of whom had links to Ruskin, were defeated by Independents, while Ludlow failed to win back his West ward seat in a subsequent by-election. The Labour candidate in the parliamentary election which followed was John Etty who came from Swindon. There was criticism of Etty for his middle class background, though Etty claimed that he had no class at all, had been a socialist since the age of 17 and had 'upheld the socialist argument in his school debating society'. Etty came bottom of the poll with 4,698 votes to 8,561 for the Liberal candidate, Moon, and 14,638 for the sitting Tory MP, Bourne. Ludlow was however returned to the city council in July after a four-year absence. A new Labour Party branch was established for the Cowley and Iffley ward, though it appears to have had no contact with the trade unionists at Morris's car factory in Cowley. These were lean years for the Oxford Labour Party and even the strong Headington ward seems to have disintegrated.

The creation of the 1931 National Government by Ramsay MacDonald was a further blow to the Oxford labour movement. The Oxford Labour Party supported MacDonald, while the Trades Council, where the communist influence was stronger, condemned the "black treachery of the Labour members who have joined or supported the so-called National Government ... We declare this National Government to be one created specifically for the purpose of wage cuts and the further degradation and starvation of the employed and unemployed. We further regard it as a huge conspiracy to economise at the expense of the working class, and all at the dictation of bankers, rentiers, millionaires and industrial magnates."

The University Labour Club also attacked the Government and elected Cole as its president in place of MacDonald. The party was again in disarray. No Labour candidate was stood in the 1931 general election, nor were candidates put forward in the subsequent local elections. In 1932, Ludlow was returned unopposed but died four months later. The Labour candidate in the by-election which followed, Edgar Smewin, a railwayman, failed to attract Ludlow's personal vote and Labour was again left without representation on the city council.

The Oxford labour movement was woken up by the arrival of a group of hunger marchers in Oxford in October 1932. The initiative was taken by the University Labour club and the University communist October club rather by the Trades Council or by the city Labour or Communist parties. An Oxford branch of the National Unemployed Workers Movement was established and the NUWM leader, Wal Hannington, spoke in Oxford twice. The city council was lobbied successfully to provide a public works programme. Patrick Gordon Walker, university academic and Labour Party member, chaired a meeting in April 1934, with the veteran campaigner Tom Mann, who was now a communist, as main speaker. It was however the growth of fascism in Oxford, with the founding of a local branch of the British Union of Fascists in February 1933, that was the catalyst for a revived militancy in the local labour movement. A Council of Action against war and fascism was established which embraced the Trades Council, the Labour Party, the University Labour and October clubs , the Friends of the Soviet Union and the Red Shirt movement. There were protest meetings and demonstrations against fascist speakers. The vice chancellor tried to ban a meeting with Ellen Wilkinson. A BUF meeting at the Town Hall with Mosley as the main speaker became violent.

John Ida, who worked at Morris's and was active in the TGWU and the Trades Council had become Labour Party secretary and in the summer of 1933 set up a series of mass meetings, door-to-door canvassing and leaflet distribution. He produced a new Labour programme for Oxford. In July 1934, there was a strike at Pressed Steel at Morris's. There was little union organisation at the plant, but the local communists appealed to the London headquarters for help and a fulltime organiser was sent to city – Abe Lazarus, who had led the strike at the Firestone tyre works in West London,

Abe Lazarus

and was known as ' Bill Firestone'. The local communist organiser, Waterhouse, set up a Solidarity Committee. Lazarus and two TGWU officials spoke at a first mass meeting, while Ida, Lazarus and Bowles of the Trades Council, who was also a communist, spoke at a second mass meeting. The Labour Party agreed to support the strike and a rally was held at St Giles'. On the eleventh day of the strike, the management gave way, guaranteeing a basic wage and recognizing trade unions within the factory. The victory had a speedy impact on the Oxford labour movement. A group of members of the strike committee led by Emrys Williams, revived the defunct Cowley branch of the Labour Party. The Headington branch was also revived under the leadership of staff members from Ruskin, Sam Smith and Fred Smith. The revival of the party in the four historic wards was much slower and for the six years up to the second world war, the Oxford Labour Party was to be dominated by members of the Cowley and Headington branches, the wards however remaining outside the Oxford parliamentary constituency. In 1933-4, the Oxford Labour Party's membership was only 120, but by 1935/6 it had grown to 225. In the 1934 council elections, Edgar Smewin was elected in West ward, while in South ward, George Clarkson, a GMWU organiser and Labour sympathiser was elected as an Independent.

The GMWU branch chairman, Ted Loynd, a former Ruskin student and communist, called for labour organisations and trade unions to work together , claiming there was 'a noble spirit of unity in the ranks'. Gordon Walker, who had become well known in the city was the Labour candidate in the general election held in November 1935. The election manifesto attacked the four years of Tory misrule and the government's rearmament programme, focusing on support for the League of Nations. It also made an explicit appeal for middle class votes, claiming that 'it is the middle class that suffers as much as anyone in the recurrent crisis of the capitalist system.' The Liberal Party, despite coming second in the previous election, for the first time did not stand a candidate so Labour drew considerable liberal support, as well as support from the recently arrived industrial workers – as the *Oxford Times* put it – ' the influx of people from places very alien from Oxford's political traditions.' Gordon Walker received 9,661 votes to Bourne's 16,306. He commented that Labour would have won if it had not rained and if Headington and Cowley, where most of the Morris's workers lived, had been included in the constituency.

It was members of the Communist Party who were most involved in both the trade union politics of Morris's and the community politics of the city. There were two significant campaigns in the city in 1935. The private developers of an estate in Cutteslowe had built a wall to separate the estate from the neighbouring council housing. The Communist Party, under Abe Lazarus's leadership, led a vigorous campaign to demolish the wall. While this campaign did not achieve its objective – the walls only being demolished by the council in 1959 following a compulsory purchase order – the campaign gave the Communist Party, and Abe Lazarus specifically, a very strong public profile. The Communist Party also supported a residents group protesting against poor conditions on a recently built private estate at Florence Park, in Cowley, where many workers at Morris's lived. The developer was a Conservative councillor, while another Conservative councillor had supplied the faulty concrete. While the protest was led by an AEU shop steward who was a Labour Party member, the support committee was led by a communist, Arthur Wynn. Local Labour Party members including Gordon Walker were also involved in the campaign. The Communist Party made an explicit link in the campaign publicity to the success of the Pressed Steel strike the previous year. The tenants went on rent strike, though this collapsed when four members of the tenants committee were evicted for rent arrears. The campaign was in effect an early example of a united front of the Trades Council the Labour Party and the Communist Party. There was new rent strikes in the area early in 1939 involving both communists and Labour Party members, with Labour activists, Richard Crossman and Frank Pakenham, being trustees of the rent strike fund.

Given this record of collaborative working, it should not be surprising that Oxford became a centre of the United Front movement, the Communist Party nationally having moved away from its Class Against Class politics, which had seen the Labour Party branded as social fascists. In June 1935, following an initiative from the Communist Party, the two parties met to discuss the possibility of some form collaboration in council elections. The communists wanted the Labour Party to stand only one candidate for the two vacant seats in Cowley ward, so their own candidate Donovan Brown, had a better chance. The proposal was supported by both the Oxford Labour Party and the Cowley and Iffley branch, despite it being pointed out that this was contrary to national Labour party rules. Many of the leading Labour Party members were sympathetic to the Communist Party and there seems to be an acknowledgement that the Communist Party was better organized in the ward than was the Labour Party. However, the ward Labour Party then changed its position and nominated two candidates for the vacancies. On the advice of the Labour Party's regional organizer, the constituency party also reversed its position. The Communist Party then withdrew its candidate, with the consequence that both Labour Party candidates were elected to the city council. The university academic, Richard Crossman was also returned for Headington and a GMWU official, W Wiltshire returned in South ward, so together with Smewin elected two years earlier in West ward, the Labour group was now five. The group was then joined by two sitting Independent councillors – George Clarkson in South ward and F Brown in Headington, taking the group total to seven. When a by- election was called in Cowley and Iffley, not unreasonably the Communist Party asked the Labour Party that this time it should withdraw its candidate in favour of the Communist candidate. Despite considerable support within the Labour Party for this suggestion, Labour insisted on standing its own candidate. Brown refused to withdraw a second time in its favour. However only the moderates within the Labour Party actually came out to support the Labour candidate. It is possible that some of the local Labour Party members actually supported Donovan Brown as there was a row between the Oxford party and the local party, with the Cowley and Iffley party claiming they should be autonomous as they were outside the Oxford parliamentary constituency. The split between Labour and the Communists had let in the Tory candidate, Sir Arthur Nelson, who received 1,104 votes to 748 for the Labour candidate, Hamilton, and 453 for the Communist, Donovan Brown.

Early in 1936, the Communist Party applied for affiliation to the Labour Party. This was supported by the Oxford Labour Party executive and by the General Committee on an overwhelming majority of 51 votes to five. When the Labour Party National Executive Committee turned down the application, the Oxford Labour Party sent a strong letter of protest and called for a national conference of the two parties to discuss a common basis for unity of action. In their annual report for the Labour Party, the chair Evan Roberts and the secretary Bessie Kirk referred to successful collaboration with the Oxford Communist Party. This led to protests, but their position was endorsed on a 35-17 vote. This however demonstrated that a significant minority of Labour Party activists in the city were unhappy about working with the communists. In July, Abe Lazarus led a communist delegation to the Labour Party executive committee to discuss electoral collaboration. This time the Labour Party agreed to stand only one candidate for the Cowley and Iffley ward. The local Cowley party was opposed to this, but fell in line with the city party, leaving the second place for the Communist Party, who this time stood Abe Lazarus. While Labour won one seat, the Tory candidate won the second seat, though Lazarus received a very creditable 1,476 votes. The Communist Party had agreed not to stand candidates where this would take votes from the Labour candidates. Labour now had 12 seats on the city council, compared with 30 Conservatives, 17 Liberals and 9 Independents.

When the Communist Party, the Socialist League and the ILP published their Unity Manifesto in January 1937, the Oxford Labour Party agreed to endorse it. Gordon Walker was concerned that if he signed personally, the Labour Party would remove their endorsement of his candidacy for the parliamentary seat, as they had already done for William Mellor of the Socialist League. He therefore consulted all the ward branches and affiliated organisations. The majority supported the manifesto, though Richard Crossman, who was leader of the Labour Group on the council, thought Gordon Walker was moving too fast and 'that there was a danger of splitting the working-class movement in Oxford'. The Oxford Party recommended that all its branches and affiliated organisations sign the Manifesto. The Headington branch however thought this was 'inadvisable' while the Central Womens' section not only opposed the Unity Manifesto, but wrote to the *Oxford Mail* to say they could no longer support Gordon Walker as parliamentary candidate.

The Oxford Labour Party agreed to set up a local Unity committee. The committee comprised Roberts, Pakenham and Prickett (respectively Labour Party chair, secretary and treasurer), Moxley and Jensen of the Trades Council and Waterhouse and Lazarus from the Communist Party. The Trades Council representatives were communist supporters if not actually members. Roberts was certainly close to the Communist Party, while Prickett as a former secretary of the Oxford Communist Party may still have been a member. The committee organised a public meeting in Oxford Town Hall on 28th May. Chaired by Gordon Walker, the speakers were James Maxton of the ILP, Johnny Campbell from the Communist

Party and William Mellor of the Socialist League. Gordon Walker appealed to Liberals to support the campaign.

During 1937, the Oxford Labour Party remained militantly left-wing. The Labour Party supported strikes at Pressed Steel and at the bus company, with Prickett and Bessie Kirk representing the party on yet another Council of Action, together with two Communist Party representatives. As Gordon Walker had previously indicated, the Labour Party was prepared to collaborate with progressive Liberals as well as with Communists. In a by-election in East ward, where Labour had never won a seat, Labour agreed to support the Liberal candidate, Honor Balfour, who had participated in anti-fascist activity. Roberts, Pakenham and Gordon Walker issued a statement saying they wished to 'advance the cause of progressive forces in the city and to avoid as far as possible any split between Liberals and Labour.' It was reported that the two parties had agreed a municipal programme. Balfour was however defeated by the Tory candidate, though she was soon elected to the council in another ward.

When Hitler invaded Austria on 12 March 1938, Richardson, the Labour Party chairman, convened a joint meeting of the Labour Party and Trades Council executive committees which established an Oxford Coordinating Committee for Peace and Democracy. The group agreed to work for the downfall of the Chamberlain government. Pakenham chaired a meeting at the Town Hall, with Lazarus as one of the speakers. The meeting was followed by a march through St Giles'. This was followed by a protest meeting at Pembroke Hall, chaired by Richardson and with Dudley Edwards from the Communist Party speaking together with Horne of the Labour League of Youth, a vicar, and Councillor Yeatman, who had been an Independent but now supported Labour. Speakers at another mass meeting included Pakenham, Roberts, Lazarus and Honor Balfour for the Liberals. Pakenham then proposed an agreement with the Liberal Party in respect of parliamentary candidatures to cover Oxford and neighbouring constituencies. This was to extend the 'popular front' agreement, previously agreed for the Banbury constituency. The new proposal was that the Liberals withdraw their candidate in Oxford while Labour would withdraw its candidate in Aylesbury in North Berkshire. It was agreed that Pakenham, Richardson and Prickett negotiate this proposal with the Liberals. There was however opposition within the Oxford Labour Party to this 'popular front' led by John Ida, who had a key role in re-establishing the Oxford Labour Party in the early 1930's. Nevertheless, the majority of the Oxford party were for the 'popular front' as well as supporting joint working with the Communists. A proposal to support the United Peace Alliance, a Communist-sponsored organization, was agreed by 21 votes to 16. There was less opposition to collaborating with the Liberals – a proposal to arrange a joint meeting with the Liberals on the international crisis was carried by 21 votes to four.

The national Labour Party was concerned at the direction the Oxford Labour Party was taking. Transport House sent a letter warning the party not to work in the 'United Front Movement', though the Oxford party recorded this as referring to the 'United and Popular Front. When the party failed to respond, Transport House threatened the party with disaffiliation if they did not withdraw from the Coordinating Committee for Peace and Democracy. Shepherd, the national agent, also complained at the Oxford's party's approach to the Aylesbury party. Prickett replied that the Oxford Labour Party needed to cooperate with local Communists or they would be cut off from many local campaigns. He claimed that 'the remarkable progress made by the whole movement in the city bears testimony to the correctness of our policy'.

In August, Robert Bourne, the Conservative MP died. The Liberal parliamentary candidate, Ivor Davies offered to withdraw in favour of 'a progressive candidate without party allegiances' if Gordon Walker also withdrew. With Hitler's invasion of Czechoslovakia, prompting the Munich crisis and the Chamberlain government's concessions to Hitler, Davies and Gordon Walker joined together to organise a protest meeting at the Town Hall. The meeting was actually chaired by the Liberal candidate for Aylesbury, MacDonald. Crossman also spoke. The platform included the Liberal academic Gilbert Murray, Abe Lazarus, Hector Prickett and at least five other Labour or independent councillors. After the meeting, Roy Harrod, a university economics don (and biographer of Keynes) took up Davies's earlier suggestion and together with Crossman and Pakenham, approached the political philosopher, A D Lindsay, who was master of Balliol College, to ask him to stand as an Independent Progressive candidate. Lindsay was a Labour Party member though he had not been active in the Oxford party. A committee was established to support his candidacy and negotiate with the Labour Party. Crossman then told Gordon Walker, who had no intention of standing down. Given Gordon Walker had been a leading supporter of the United Front, he clearly felt betrayed that his colleagues had gone behind his back to do a deal with the Liberals. Gordon Walker in his diary considered that the initiative was prompted by Crossman's jealously of his candidacy. Prickett and Richardson both supported a popular front candidacy. Edgar Smewin, the longest serving Labour councillor, did not. A series of meetings with Transport House officials led to a changed position as the national Labour Party, which having originally supported Gordon Walker's refusal to stand down, agreed to leave the decision to the local party. After a series of fraught meetings and negotiations, the Oxford Labour Party decided, on a vote of 48 to 12, to withdraw Gordon Walker's candidacy. Lindsay agreed not to take the Labour whip if elected. Pakenham personally paid off the Liberal Party's expenses of £350 and Ivor Davies withdrew his candidacy, leaving a straight fight between A D Lindsay and the Conservative candidate, Quintin Hogg. The alliance supporting Lindsay was a strange one, ranging from the Communist Party to dissident Conservatives including Randolph Churchill, Harold Macmillan, the radical Liberal, Megan Lloyd-George and even a student called Edward Heath. Lindsay expected to win, failing to understand why anybody could vote against him. Hogg was returned with a vote of 15,797 to Lindsay's 12,363.

The Oxford Labour Party was required by the Labour Party national executive to hold an inquest on the by-election. This was attended by Hugh Dalton as well as Shepherd, the national agent, and NEC member, George Latham. Pakenham argued that Lindsay would have won if they had support if the national party. Smewin commented that the withdrawal of Gordon Walker had been engineered by 'Communists on one side and the University on the other.' The Oxford party gave a commitment to support a Labour parliamentary candidate in the future. In January 1939, the party adopted a new candidate. Gordon Walker received eight nominations; Pakenham four. Pakenham argued that following the by-election Gordon Walker was no longer electable. Pakenham was then adopted by 43 votes to 11 for Gordon Walker. The NEC refused to endorse Pakenham unless the Oxford party gave assurances not to make deals with other parties or withdraw from the next election contest. Pakenham refused to agree to these conditions. The Oxford Labour Party was still pursuing a 'popular front' course and was still negotiating with the Liberals. Richardson and Prickett had apparently been attending meetings at A D Lindsay's house with Liberals and Independents and drawing up a joint programme. Smewin tried to stop the meetings but was defeated by 24 votes to six. When the NEC expelled Stafford Cripps for his popular front activities, Cripps was invited to speak in Oxford. The NEC again threatened to disaffiliate the Oxford Labour Party if it continued to support the Left Book Club and the Popular Front. The Oxford party then supported a Popular Front conference held at Lindsay's house at Balliol, which had delegates from ten constituencies Crossman was sent to the national conference to support Cripps.

The NEC then decided to endorse Pakenham after all. Prickett was offered the position of paid agent and Pakenham donated £150 to the fund for his salary. Prickett however decided to turn down the offer and instead resigned from the Labour Party and publicly joined the Communist Party. There was no evidence that Prickett had ever left the Communist Party, having been secretary of the Oxford communists in the 1920s. The Communist Party had recently decided that its members within the Labour Party should come into the open. The Oxford Party chairman, Richardson, who had supported the Communist Party, even if he was not a paid up member, moved away from the city at the same time. Within two months the country was at war. The Oxford party focused on ensuring Labour representation on wartime organisations such as the Evacuees Coordination Committee and the Citizens Advice Bureau, and the years of rebellion seem to have come to an end.

The Oxford Labour Party and the Working Class

The Labour Party did not develop an effective political base in Oxford until the late 1920s, and even then, it was not the dominant factor in working class politics in the city. In the 1920s, trade union movement in Oxford was still largely based on the old craft unions such as the printers with their traditional liberal values. The initiative to form a Labour Party in Oxford in 1920 was taken not by trade unionists but by middle class socialist sympathisers such as A J Carlyle. Support from trade unionists was far from solid and the party was easily wrecked by the intervention of communists, led by the postal worker, Wigington, who made a strange alliance with Liberal trade unionists to kill the Oxford Labour Party at its birth, and at the same time to create divisions in the Trades Council that split the labour movement in the city for a decade. The Labour Party in Oxford in the 1920s was not a party in the organised sense, but a group of constantly feuding individuals of diverse backgrounds. To the few local Labour leaders who had the support of the working-class electorate, the most prominent of whom was Fred Ludlow, the local labour movement was more of an embarrassment than a support. The failure of Labour in Oxford in the early 1920s was also due to the Liberal revival based on the enigmatic figure of Frank Gray. Gray became a working-class hero in the city and was on friendly terms with many of Oxford's leading trade unionists. While Gray was active in the city, the Labour Party stood no hope of winning working-class support in a parliamentary contest. It is significant that as late as 1938, the Labour Party was to claim Gray's inheritance. Yet, the Oxford Labour Party failed to recognise that Gray succeeded because he was local, and repeatedly made the mistake of choosing middle-class candidates – Kenneth Lindsay in 1924, John Etty in 1929 and Gordon Walker in 1935. Many of Labour's candidates in the municipal elections in the 1920s had university connections and could easily be attacked by Liberals and Tories alike as 'rich socialists'. Throughout the 1920s and early 1930s, the Tories and Liberals kept substantial working-class support, especially in the East ward, where no Labour candidate was successful until after the Second World War.

The General Strike was not a central event in Oxford in the development of the local labour movement, though it is often a focus of attention because so many future Labour leaders, then at the university, served their political apprenticeship in that hectic week. The Labour Party was weak in Oxford in 1926 and many leading trade unionists in the city, such as Trades Council president, Bowles, were communists. During the strike, the Trades Council was heavily dependent on assistance from sympathisers in the university and at Ruskin.

The Oxford Labour Party was in the early stages of recovery when it was shaken by the defection of the Labour Leaders, MacDonald, Snowden and Thomas in 1931. Defectors to MacDonald's National Labour Party included the first Labour parliamentary candidate in the city, Kenneth Lindsay, and the former municipal candidate, Godfrey Elton, who was raised to a peerage by MacDonald. There was no Labour candidate in the ensuing parliamentary election in Oxford. The short-lived regeneration of the local Labour Party had been based on the traditional alliance of middle class sympathisers and trade unionists from established industries and did not have the political base needed to survive the crisis.

The revival of the party after 1934 was primarily a product of the development of trade unionism at the Cowley factories. Trade unionism had been slow to emerge at Cowley and it was only with the 1934 strike that the Labour movement began to build up a strong organisation in the city. The role played by the Communist Party, under the leadership of Abe Lazarus, in the Pressed Steel strike and the linked struggles in Florence Park and Cutteslowe, was to secure for it an influential and respected role in the local labour movement. It was the Communist Party's strength and the Labour Party's comparative lack of a political base in the Cowley area, that was the basis for the United Front developments in Oxford in the later 1930's

Though the Labour Party revival was initiated by Cowley workers such as John Ida, the party soon attracted a new generation of academic sympathisers, such as Richard Crossman, Patrick Gordon Walker and Frank Pakenham, all of whom were to use Oxford Labour politics as a stepping stone into national politics and to serve in Harold Wilson's cabinet. These academics shared the interest of the Communist Party in opposing the growing fascist movement, and though the Labour Party gradually developed its role in municipal politics, the real excitement in local labour politics was centred on the fight against fascism at home and abroad. Crossman, while leader of the Labour group on the city council, also wrote regularly for the *New Statesman*. Pakenham, who had many contacts in national politics, tended to use the city council as a platform for wider issues. It was Gordon Walker who, though never a councillor, was most consistent in his commitment to campaigning on local issues such as housing and consequently was closest to the local Labour trade unionists.

The 1938 by-election represented the apogee of the Lazarus/Crossman/Pakenham dominance of the local labour movement. By 1938, the Oxford Labour Party was effectively controlled by communists and communist sympathisers. The party secretary, Hector Prickett, worked in the Communist Party's interests, and may have retained his Communist Party membership throughout his tenure of office in the Oxford Labour Party. He was supported by the majority of his Labour Party colleagues, including the chair, Richardson, Crossman and Pakenham, in doing so. Given the extent to which the Oxford Party was dominated by this communist-academic alliance, the party's stance in the by-election is not surprising. By 1938, the Oxford party had a considerable record of United Front and Popular Front activity, and in the atmosphere of Munich, this was logically extended into an electoral alliance, despite opposition from many of the Labour Party's working-class members. This development was assisted by the prevarication of the national leadership of the Labour Party. Gordon Walker, who had strongly supported the United Front was however cautious about extending this alliance to include the Liberal Party.

To communists and academics alike, resistance to international fascism was the all-important issue and Gordon Walker was jettisoned in favour of a progressive academic, A D Lindsay, who was largely unknown outside university circles. The by-election was a fight between two University dons which was only of limited relevance to the majority of the city's population. The extent to which the local Labour leadership was distanced from the working-class electorate they claimed to represent was the fact that they, and Lindsay, failed to believe anybody could vote against them. When Lindsay was defeated, neither Pakenham or his colleagues could recognise their mistake. With the by-election over, the party continued its Popular Front activities – Pakenham became parliamentary candidate, the party courted disaffiliation by the NEC, and several working-class activists in the party either resigned or became inactive. The Oxford Labour Party may have been dynamic and exciting but it was far from being the united working-class party which it claimed to be. It nevertheless provides an interesting case study of the relationship between communists and the Labour Party.

The Labour Party and the Law on Strikes: From Taff Vale 1901 to the 2016 Trade Union Act, via In Place of Strife 1969

Dave Lyddon

For most of the Labour Party's history, one constant feature has been to promote or pass statutes to reverse court judgments, or repeal legislation, that inhibited the right to strike. In this respect, it acted as the political wing of the labour movement. This position generally operated from its 1900 foundation, under the auspices of the Trades Union Congress (TUC), until the late 1980s. It came under strain with Labour's *In Place of Strife* White Paper in 1969, but this was a more mixed episode than popular accounts suggest. The major break, accepting the succession of Tory laws from 1980, occurred after the 1987 general election, under the leadership of Neil Kinnock (1983–92), and was consolidated by Tony Blair (1994–2007). The 2017 Labour election manifesto's proposal to repeal the Tory government's 2016 Trade Union Act represents the first crack in this latter-day bi-partisan consensus.

From Taff Vale to the 1927 Act

Strike law in the UK has always been politically contested as there is no legal 'right to strike'. Trade unions' ability to function has had to be accommodated within the existing system of 'common [judge-made] law'. Unions ceased to be unlawful associations in 1871, and Parliament in 1875 removed the remaining criminal liability from strikes, known from that time as 'trade disputes', though picketing has remained subject to criminal sanctions. After 1875, the courts developed civil liability against unions through 'torts' (civil wrongs other than breach of contract).[1] From 1893 to 1901 a series of judgments 'whittled away' the unions' ability to strike.[2] In 1901 the highest court (the House of Lords, now the Supreme Court) upheld, in the *Taff Vale* judgment, that a union could be sued for tort; other unions then suffered this fate. Sidney and Beatrice Webb estimated that at least £200,000 was spent in damages and legal expenses from judgments against unions and officials during this period of court cases against them.[3] The 1906 Trade Disputes Act (TDA), passed by the landslide Liberal government, under pressure from the TUC and the infant Labour Party, granted unions 'immunity' against legal liability for torts committed 'in contemplation or furtherance of a trade dispute', reversing the effects of adverse court judgments.

---

1   Lord Wedderburn, *The Worker and the Law* (Harmondsworth, 1986; 3rd edn), pp.16–25. The main relevant torts now are inducement of breach of contract, interference with economic interests, civil conspiracy to injure, civil intimidation. Anyone organising or threatening a strike, for example, commits the tort of inducing a breach of contracts of employment.
2   B C Roberts, *The Trades Union Congress, 1868–1921* (London, 1958), p.164.
3   Sidney and Beatrice Webb, *The History of Trade Unionism* (London, 1920), p.602.

Trade disputes were defined very broadly to encompass secondary action and inter-union disputes.[4] The TDA was the trade unions' *Magna Carta*.

Lewis Minkin has argued that the 'protection and advancement of labour's industrial interests was ... the most basic and unifying purpose of the Labour Party'.[5] After the 1906 TDA, there followed the 1913 Trade Union Act, which reversed the *Osborne* judgment (1910) and established how unions could lawfully spend money on political purposes. But when the Labour Party formed its first minority government (1924), its view of 'the national interest' led it to threaten to use the 1920 Emergency Powers Act during high-profile transport strikes. As a result, a more formal differentiation (and autonomy) developed not only between the Labour Party and the TUC (abandoning their joint departments) but also between Labour and its affiliated unions. Minkin suggests that in the late 1920s and early 1930s there was a 'clarification' of many of the 'understandings, obligations and prudential guidelines which regulated the relationship – in effect its "rules"'.[6]

'Industrial freedom', through collective organisation, was of 'primary' importance to unions. Having been

> secured ... in the face of hostility from employers, the judiciary and, on
> occasion, the Government and legislature, it was guarded against threats or
> incursions from any source. Thus, in a Party committed to defending the union
> capacity to organise, bargain, regulate and activate industrial sanctions
> against employers, it was outside permissible bounds ... that the Party should
> restrict what it had been created to protect.[7]

In the wake of the unsuccessful 1926 General Strike in support of the miners, the Conservative government passed the 1927 Trade Disputes and Trade Unions Act (TDTUA). Among its many provisions, which included weakening the financial base of the Labour Party, it made strikes against the government and most secondary strikes 'illegal' and created a new criminal offence (never prosecuted) of furthering an illegal strike; such strikes lost their immunity against civil action.[8] The Act also created new picketing offences. The TUC reported of its efforts against the Bill: 'Never has so large a campaign received so little attention'.[9] Speaking for Labour during the Bill's second reading, J R Clynes promised: 'it will be the duty of the Opposition ..., when in the natural order of things it becomes a Government, no matter in what form this Bill may pass, to repeal that Act ... because such an Act ...

---

4 John Saville, 'The Trade Disputes Act of 1906', *Historical Studies in Industrial Relations (HSIR)*, 1 (1996), pp.11–45.
5 Lewis Minkin, *The Contentious Alliance. Trade unions and the Labour Party* (Edinburgh, 1991), p.11.
6 Minkin, *Contentious Alliance*, p.26.
7 Minkin, *Contentious Alliance*, pp. 27–28 (emphasis in original).
8 Adrian Williamson, 'The Trade Disputes and Trade Unions Act 1927 reconsidered', *HSIR*, 37, 2016, pp.33–82.
9 Trades Union Congress (TUC), *Annual Report 1927*, pp.248–259.

would be a malignant endeavour on the part of the Government to back up organised capital in the struggles with organised labour'.[10] This pledge was 'a strongly unifying commitment'.[11]

The 1929 minority Labour government, under pressure from the TUC, tried to restore the pre-1927 position, but the Liberals were unable to support this, so an amending Bill was presented. When this reached committee stage, the Liberals amended it in such a way that, according to the TUC, 'any kind of strike, for whatever object, should become illegal if at any point its effect was to hold up the community'. This was even worse than the 1927 Act, so the TUC General Council prevailed upon the government to withdraw the Bill.[12]

The 1945 Government

The 1945 majority Labour government repealed the Act in 1946, 'simply, brusquely, triumphantly':[13] 'The Trade Disputes and Trade Unions Act ... is hereby repealed, and, subject to the transitional provisions ... every enactment and rule of law amended or otherwise affected by that Act shall ... have effect as if the Act of 1927 had not been passed.'[14] Ernest Bevin, former general secretary of the Transport and General Workers' Union (TGWU) and Minister of Labour in the wartime coalition government but by now Labour's foreign secretary, could not resist speaking in the debate on the second reading: 'If ever there was a class Act, this was one.' The Tories had 'cast the trade unions ... [as] enemies of the State, and while as an individual I have been a trade union leader for 20 years, I never have been an enemy of the State. I have been as big a constitutionalist as any Member on the other side of the House, and I am fighting to remove the stigma which the Tory Party in 1927 put upon me, as the leader of a trade union'.[15]

Denis Pritt, expelled from the Labour Party in 1940, while an MP, but by now sitting as an Independent Labour member, supported the government in the debate, though he had (unsuccessfully) drafted some amendments for consideration.[16] He later criticised Labour for not going beyond the pre-1927 legal position, especially regarding the status of general strikes: 'the deliberate and cowardly maintenance of all the old uncertainties and weaknesses of the law, calculated to cripple resolute action by the trade union and working-class movement at some critical moment'.[17] By contrast, Terence Donovan (later, as Lord Donovan of the Court of Appeal, the chair of the 1965–68 royal commission), making his maiden speech as a Labour MP,

---

10 House of Commons Debates, 2 May 1927, col.1340.
11 Minkin, *Contentious Alliance*, p.11.
12 TUC, *Annual Report 1931*, pp.253–5; *The Times*, 4 March 1931.
13 Charles Loch Mowat, *Britain between the Wars 1918–1940* (London, 1956), p.337.
14 Trade Disputes and Trade Unions Act 1946, s.1.
15 House of Commons Debates, 13 February 1946, cols 411, 399.
16 D N Pritt, *Labour Government, 1945–51* (London, 1963), p.52.
17 D N Pritt, *Law, Class and Society, Book One: Employers, workers and trade unions* (1970), p.93.

argued: 'whether there is ever a general strike again will not depend on whether there is a Statute allowing it or prohibiting it or leaving it doubtful as to whether it is legal or illegal; it will depend on whether the endurance of our people has been strained beyond breaking point by economic injustice'.[18]

Demanding the Repeal of Order 1305

Yet the same 1945 Labour government, with TUC support, had continued the wartime Order 1305,[19] under which disputes had to be reported to the Ministry of Labour and strikes 'prohibited' for 21 days. If a dispute could not be conciliated it was sent to arbitration, though there was no interference in existing negotiating machinery. Introduced by Bevin in 1940, this followed 'closely the structure, and indeed the wording' of the Munitions of War Act 1915, though, unlike this, it applied to all industries.[20] Despite 109 prosecutions and 6,300 workers prosecuted for breach of this during the Second World War, the number of strikes (particularly in coalmining) rose every year from 1940 to 1945, more than doubling overall.[21] The government was decidedly reluctant to institute criminal prosecutions in peacetime

18 House of Commons Debates, 13 February 1946, col.420.
19 Conditions of Employment and National Arbitration Order, 1940.
20 Pritt, *Employers, workers and trade unions*, p.88.

and eventually only did so to deal with Communist industrial militancy. In late 1950, ten gas fitters were fined but not imprisoned; then in April 1951 seven dockers were tried but acquitted, by which time a replacement arbitration order (without sanctions) was being drafted.[22] Labour governments also declared states of emergency, allowing the use of troops, during certain strikes.[23]

In Place of Strife: Mixed Messages

When, after thirteen years, Labour returned to government under Harold Wilson in October 1964, it continued to support a wide freedom to strike while threatening sanctions against strikes in certain instances. It repealed the section of the 1963 Contracts of Employment Act that broke continuity of service for workers who had been on strike.[24] Labour also reversed the effect of the *Rookes* v *Barnard* (1964) case – which had resulted in three union officials paying £4,000 damages – by the 1965 Trade Disputes Act (against great opposition in the Tory-dominated House of Lords).[25] Within weeks of the 1964 election the TUC had agreed to an inquiry (a royal commission) into 'trade unions and their place in the law and national

Barbara Castle

affairs', its particular concern being the consequences of another court case, *Stratford* v. *Lindley* (1964).[26] Against this record must be set Labour's 1966 Prices and Incomes Act, which contained (without TUC opposition) reserve criminal sanctions (fines – never used) in the event of strikes to force wage rises banned by statutory incomes policy.[27]

During the late 1960s the British industrial relations problem was seen as 'unconstitutional strikes' (in breach of disputes procedures), which were usually also unofficial, at a time of increasing industrial action outside coalmining. In this atmosphere, the 1968 report of the Donovan Commission made two important proposals on strikes.[28] Under the initiative of Barbara Castle, secretary of state at the Department of Employment and Productivity (DEP), Labour's January 1969 White

21 Nina Fishman, '"A vital element in industrial relations": A reassessment of Order 1305, 1940–51', *HSIR*, 8 (1999), pp.43–86.
22 Fishman, 'A vital element in industrial relations', especially pp.51–71.
23 Keith Jeffrey and Peter Hennessy, *States of Emergency. British governments and strikebreaking since 1919* (London, 1983), pp.143–221 for 1945–51; Gillian Morris, *Strikes in Essential Services* (London, 1986), pp.100–106.
24 Redundancy Payments Act 1965, s.37.
25 *The Times*, 22 January, 3 and 20 August, 1965.
26 *The Times*, 26 November 1964.
27 Prices and Incomes Act 1966, s.16(4). Barbara Castle later said this section was not 'penal legislation to undermine and weaken the unions' but 'reserve powers' where 'there was deliberate intent to pressurise an employer into committing an offence': *The Times*, 26 June 1968.

Paper, *In Place of Strife* (*IPOS*) rejected the Donovan commission's majority view to *remove* immunity from unofficial strike leaders inducing breach of contract: 'the Government does not believe this would improve matters'.[29] It did agree, though, with the recommendation to reverse *Stratford* v *Lindley* (1964): 'inducement of breach of a commercial contract in the circumstances of a trade dispute should be protected in the same way as the inducement of a breach of a contract of employment.' It elaborated: 'The alternative is to outlaw sympathetic action. But *trade unions have a long tradition of relying on the solidarity of union members working in different places, and it would be wrong to attach legal penalties*'.[30]

IPOS began: 'There are necessarily conflicts of interest in industry. The objective of our industrial relations system should be to direct the forces producing conflict towards constructive ends.'[31] But this system had 'serious defects' and without action to remedy these, 'conflict in British industry will often be damaging and anti-social'. The White Paper's proposals (many of which followed Donovan) included some to 'help to contain the destructive expression of industrial conflict'.[32] These were the three 'penal clauses' so politically toxic they nearly brought down the government. Two of them – conciliation pauses (or 'cooling-off' periods) and ballots – had been rejected by Donovan earlier, as likely to be ineffective and possibly even counter-productive. The presence of these clauses reflected Labour's dilemma between being a party rooted in the unions (and upholding their freedom) and being the governing party (and needing to steal a march on the Tories). So there was 'a discretionary reserve power to secure a 'conciliation pause' [of 28 days] in unconstitutional strikes' – to be used when 'the effects were likely to be serious' and only after DEP conciliation had been tried. But, at the same time, *IPOS* argued that '*in many strikes the employer is at fault*' and should '*withdraw the offending action* till adequate discussion had taken place'[33] – thus supporting a *status quo* clause, something then conspicuously lacking in the engineering industry procedure agreement. Second, where a 'major official strike' was called, there should be a 'discretionary power' to require the union(s) to hold a ballot (according to a union's own rules) where there was 'a serious threat to the economy and public interest' and doubt that the strike commanded members' support.[34] Third, the proposed Commission on Industrial Relations could make recommendations in unresolved inter-union disputes.[35]

---

28 *Royal Commission on Trade Unions and Employers' Associations, 1965–1968, Report*, Cmnd 3623 (London, 1968) (Donovan Report).

29 *In Place of Strife. A policy for industrial relations* (*IPOS*), Cmnd 3888 (London, 1969), para.88; see Donovan Report, paras 798–801, 804.

30 *IPOS*, para.100 (emphasis added); see Donovan Report, paras 893–894.

31 *IPOS*, para.1.

32 *IPOS*, paras 2–3.

33 *IPOS*, paras 93–94 (emphasis added).

34 *IPOS*, para.98.

35 *IPOS*, para.60.

If these measures were defied, an 'Industrial Board' could impose 'financial penalties': on employers (for refusal to recognise a recommended union), unions or individual strikers, as appropriate – in the last, through attachment of earnings orders, thus ruling out imprisonment for non-payment.[36] In March 1969, the House of Commons divided 224–62 to approve the White Paper as the basis for legislation, with the Tories tactically abstaining while 55 Labour MPs voted against and 'about 42' abstained.[37] A short Bill was proposed in April, retaining two of the penal clauses.[38] Opposition to fines was deep-rooted: it brought 'the taint of criminality' to trade unions.[39] The TUC argued that 'the imposition of fines in industrial relations would make it possible to widen their use in future'[40] while engineering union president Hugh Scanlon made it clear that 'the Trade Union Movement would see to it that the fines were paid by sympathisers of the men concerned'.[41]

Two important sets of unofficial strikes against *IPOS* (on 27 February and 1 May) broke new ground as political strikes against the government.[42] Against this background, the conflict within the Parliamentary Labour Party (PLP) reflected the tension between Labour's traditional support for trade union freedom and the government's wider agenda. Douglas Houghton, PLP chair in 1969, had been general secretary of the tax officers' union: 'His attitude was identical with that of the moderate progressive members of the TUC General Council, of which he had himself for eight years been a member ... he knew the need for trade union reform but believed that the Donovan ... approach was ... correct ... and Barbara Castle's ... misguided' and he eventually said so.[43] Bob Mellish, right-wing former TGWU official and also against the penal clauses, was the newly appointed chief whip who told the Cabinet in June that they could not carry the parliamentary party. This intervention saw any remaining Cabinet support for Wilson and Castle drain away.

Labour then opposed the Tories' 1970 Industrial Relations (IR) Bill in Parliament, with Castle a leading spokesperson in this endeavour. Despite superficial similarities between *IPOS* and the IR Bill, there was a huge gulf between Labour's limited legal tinkering and the Tories' comprehensive effort to confine unions in a legal straitjacket. Hugh Clegg, the principal author of the Donovan Report, saw the 1971 IR Act as 'the most dramatic attempt by any British government to impose a master-

---

36 *IPOS*, para.62.
37 House of Commons Debates, 3 March 1969, columns 36–166; Andrew Alexander and Alan Watkins, *The Making of the Prime Minister, 1970* (London, 1970), p.141.
38 See, for example, TUC, *Annual Report 1969*, p.211; pp.202–225 for negotiations with government after Donovan and over *IPOS*.
39 Quoted in Kenneth O Morgan, *Britain since 1945. The people's peace* (Oxford, 2001), p.301.
40 TUC, *Annual Report 1969*, p.212.
41 Richard Tyler, '"Victims of our history"? Barbara Castle and In Place of Strife', *Contemporary British History*, 20:3 (2006), p.472.
42 John McIlroy and Alan Campbell, 'Organizing the militants: The Liaison Committee for the Defence of Trade Unions, 1966–1979', *British Journal of Industrial Relations*, 37:1 (1999), pp.1–31.
43 See Peter Jenkins, *The Battle of Downing Street* (London, 1970), for a blow-by-blow account of *IPOS*; p.118 for quote.

plan for industrial relations'.[44] During the debates on the Bill, Castle made the following (possibly unscripted) remark: 'speaking as a woman, I think that the strike weapon is essentially a masculine device. It is crude, it is clumsy and it is often inefficient.' She continued: 'Let me also add, speaking as a product of this day and age, that it is an instrument which men and women of all sections of society have been driven to use'.[45] Hardly the most spirited defence but, nevertheless, an acceptance of the necessity for strikes.

The 1970s

When Labour, which had pledged to repeal the IR Act, did so in 1974, following the Tory election defeat, its minority government was thwarted in the attempt to widen the scope of lawful secondary action (as intended in *IPOS*); it succeeded in 1976 by which time it had a small majority.[46] It did, though, re-enact the IR Act's provisions on unfair dismissal. So an employer who sacked all workers taking part in a strike would not face unfair dismissal claims, which could only happen if strikers were dismissed selectively.[47] There had been no legal remedy (however limited) for dismissal of strikers (for breach of contract) before 1971 and the Donovan Report had considered at length the question whether strikes 'should merely suspend the contract of employment without breaking it, or terminating it'. It concluded that any such move should not be made until deliberations by 'an expert Committee'.[48] *IPOS* had had nothing to say on this fundamental question. The legality of strikes was still cast in terms of immunity from the common law, and only strike organisers, not strikers themselves, were protected. The continuing lack of legal constraints in sacking whole workforces was to prove an important weapon for employers facing strikes in the 1980s and 1990s.

Picketing had played an important role in the coalmining, building and docks strikes of 1972.[49] Responding to these, and to recent court cases, the TUC drew up detailed proposals, including new rights for pickets to stop vehicles, for inclusion in the Employment Protection Bill of 1975: 'Pickets should have the right to "obstruct" the highway for a reasonable period ... to effect the purpose of communicating or obtaining information or peacefully persuading not to work'.[50] Because of strong Home Office and police objections, the government did not concede this and a backbench attempt to amend the Bill failed.[51]

44 Hugh Clegg, *The System of Industrial Relations in Great Britain* (Oxford, 1976; 3rd edn), p.501.
45 House of Commons Debates, 14 December 1970, col.1003.
46 Trade Union and Labour Relations Act (TULRA) 1974; Trade Union and Labour Relations (Amendment) Act 1976.
47 Keith Ewing, *The Right to Strike* (Oxford, 1991), pp.40–44.
48 Donovan Report, paras 942, 952.
49 Ralph Darlington and Dave Lyddon, *Glorious Summer. Class Struggle in Britain 1972* (London, 2001).
50 TUC, *Annual Report 1975*, pp.79–80.
51 Wedderburn, *Worker and the Law*, p.544; *The Times*, 31 July 1975.

Despite increasing union disaffection with the later stages of the Social Contract incomes policy, on 14 February 1979 (at the height of the so-called 'Winter of Discontent') the TUC and the Labour government issued a joint statement, which included 'improving industrial relations'. There was 'a strong recommendation that union rules should provide for strike ballots ... at the discretion of the union'. An accompanying TUC guide advised that, 'save in exceptional circumstances', unions should 'confine picketing to premises of the parties to the dispute or the premises of suppliers and customers of those parties' – still a very broad view of picketing. [52]

Tory Laws and the Road to New Labour

Strike ballots and restraints on picketing and were to be integral features of the Conservatives' six statutes, passed between 1980 and 1993, which progressively narrowed a lawful 'trade dispute'.[53] This sustained onslaught was only made possible by the unprecedented sequence of four Tory election victories, aided by the defection of Labour MPs in 1981 to establish the Social Democratic Party, which split the anti-Tory vote. The 1980 Act removed immunity from most secondary action and strikes other than over terms and conditions. Secondary picketing lost immunity. A maximum of six pickets was recommended in a 1980 code of practice. The 1982 Act significantly narrowed a lawful trade dispute and opened up unions to tort proceedings (injunctions and damages) in their own name, if certain actions had been authorised or endorsed; in practice, injunctions have caused most problems.[54] The Act also relaxed the criteria for avoiding unfair dismissal claims by allowing some selectivity in the dismissal of strikers and selective re-engagement, after three months, of dismissed strikers.[55] Workplace ballots for official strikes were introduced in 1984, replaced by postal ballots, with onerous notice requirements, in 1993. The 1988 Act made industrial action to establish or maintain a closed shop unlawful and created a right not to be 'unjustifiably disciplined' by a union – for refusing to strike, for example. The 1990 Act removed protection from all secondary action and introduced union liability for unofficial action, requiring union written 'repudiation'.

Labour promised repeal of the 1980 and 1982 Acts in its 1983 election manifesto.[56] There was some retreat from the traditional position of blanket repeal of hostile laws when, in 1986, a TUC–Labour Party Liaison Committee statement accepted the 1984

---

52 TUC, *Annual Report 1979*, pp.273–274; TUC and the Government, *The Economy, the Government and Trade Union Responsibilities: Joint Statement*, in TUC, *Annual Report 1979*, p.393, para 13; TUC Guide, Conduct of Industrial Disputes, in TUC, *Annual Report 1979*, pp.400–401, paras 5 and 9.

53 The 1980, 1982, 1988 and 1990 Employment Acts, 1984 Trade Union Act, and 1993 Trade Union Reform and Employment Rights Act. The first five, and earlier relevant legislation, were combined into the Trade Union and Labour Relations (Consolidation) Act 1992, TULR(C)A. Relevant sections of later statutes, such as the 1993 Act and the 2016 Trade Union Act, amend TULR(C)A.

54 Wedderburn, *Worker and the Law*, p.636, Table 1, identifies the common law torts, the immunities under TULRA 1974–76, and restrictions of these under 1980 and 1982 Employment Acts.

55 Ewing, *Right to Strike*, pp.44–46.

56 Minkin, *Contentious Alliance*, 1991, p.435.

Act's principle of secret ballots before official strikes (repeated in the 1987 manifesto); though a 1986 TUC Congress resolution pointedly excluded ballots before non-strike action. But the joint statement also proposed *widening* rights to picket and prohibiting *ex parte* (without notice) injunctions.[57] After the 1987 election defeat, Labour launched its fateful wide-ranging 'Policy Review'. By 1990 the Labour leadership under Kinnock had secured what Minkin has called a 'profound break' and a 'historic shift' in its policy on the law concerning industrial action. It 'transcended ninety years of history and overcame what seemed an impossible barrier in the form of ninety per cent of the Party Conference votes'.[58]

In the late 1980s Labour and the TUC were more actively embracing an agenda of individual employment rights, seeing the European Social Charter as a lifeline in the hostile climate created by successive Tory governments. Collective rights, though, were still central for most unions. In 1989 the TUC's priorities included stopping employers sacking strikers and blocking companies from restructuring to make strikes unlawful (as happened with News International in 1986–87). The September 1989 Congress went further and agreed with the TGWU call for repeal of the Tory laws and a new framework enshrining the 'right to strike including immunity in tort'.[59] This position was out of line with the Labour leadership's important understandings with TUC officials to change policy on industrial action.[60] To limit damage to Labour's electoral prospects (the driver of these changes on strike law), union concessions were forced through in time for the Labour conference a few weeks later: in return for specialist labour courts (without the power to sequestrate a union's entire assets), a union would remain liable for unlawful action.[61]

From New Labour to a Break in the Consensus

By 1992, Labour's election manifesto could boast: 'There will be no return to the trade union legislation of the 1970s. Ballots before strikes and for union elections will stay. There will be no mass or flying pickets'.[62] This prefigured the 1997 New Labour programme, which now also rejected secondary action (marking a definitive break with Donovan and *IPOS*), and the Labour government's 1998 *Fairness at Work* White Paper.[63] Despite the manoeuvring of TUC officials, though, the TUC congress

---

57 TUC, *Annual Report 1986*, pp.395–409 for TUC–Labour Party Liaison Committee, 'People at Work: New Rights, New Responsibilities'; pp.680–681 for TUC resolution. Labour Party, *Britain Will Win with Labour* (London, 1987); Minkin, *Contentious Alliance*, pp.435–437.
58 Minkin, *Contentious Alliance*, pp.623–624.
59 TUC, *Annual Report 1989*, pp.45–48, 'Employment Law: TUC Priorities'; pp.576–578 for resolution.
60 Minkin, *Contentious Alliance*, pp.469–472.
61 Colin Hughes and Patrick Wintour, *Labour Rebuilt. The new model party* (London, 1990), pp.143–152. At this stage, Labour opposed Tory proposals on unofficial strikes: John McIlroy, *The Permanent Revolution? Conservative law and the trade unions* (Nottingham, 1991), p.180.
62 Labour Party, *It's Time to Get Britain Working Again*, London, 1992.
63 Labour Party, *New Labour because Britain Deserves Better*, London, 1997; Department of Trade and Industry (DTI), *Fairness at Work*, Cm 3968, London, 1998.

majority was generally still for repeal of the Tory laws.[64] But Labour (with the unions, reluctantly or otherwise, in tow) had turned a corner, just as the British strike experience had been totally transformed by years of 'coercive pacification'.[65] The 1980s was a period of transition from the historically high strike incidence of the 1960s and 1970s, averaging 2,520 strikes annually, to less than one-tenth of that number from 1992 onwards. This collapse was concentrated in unofficial strikes (some 95 per cent of the total in the 1960s and 1970s), which were not even exposed to legislation until January 1991. The most strike-prone industries (coalmining, motor vehicles, shipbuilding and the docks) were all subject to radical product market restructuring in the 1980s, involving massive job loss and major changes in working practices. Here and in many other industries, there was 'class struggle from above', aided by a deep economic recession, draconian disciplinary codes against many workers, and mass policing of major strikes in protest. Employers' tactical use of court injunctions during strikes reinforced many manual workers' labour market weakness.[66]

Back in government in 1997, Labour, in its 1999 Employment Relations Act, amended an onerous requirement of the 1993 Act, which required unions to specify the workers they intended to ballot; where these could not be readily identified, the union had to provide names. But while Labour's amendment now preserved union members' anonymity, 'The courts have interpreted the provisions as requiring unions to attach detailed matrices to their notices identifying the number and grade of their members at each workplace involved in the dispute'.[67] Labour did, though, introduce an eight-week period of 'protected industrial action' for official strikers, during which their mass dismissal would be deemed unfair; this was extended to 12 weeks in 2004.[68] Unofficial strikers remained unprotected, as shown by the mass sackings at Gate Gourmet (based at Heathrow airport) in August 2005. This dispute led that year's Labour Party conference to support secondary action.

64 See TUC, *Annual Report 1994*, composite resolution C4; TUC, *Congress Report 1995*, composite C12; TUC, *Congress Report 1996*, composite C11.
65 Richard Hyman, *Strikes*, (London, 1989; 4th edn), pp.199–200.
66 See Dave Lyddon, 'The changing pattern of UK strikes, 1964–2014', *Employee Relations*, 37:6 (2015), pp.733–745; Dave Lyddon, 'Why trade union legislation and the Labour Party are not responsible for the decline in strike activity', *International Socialism*, 158 (2018), pp.197–221.
67 DTI, *Review of the Employment Relations Act 1999* (London, 2003), para.3.26.
68 TULR(C)A, s.238A.

Tony Woodley, TGWU general secretary, explained 'We are not calling for wildcat action ... [or] flying pickets.' A ballot would be needed and only when there was 'a close connection between those involved'. Trade and Industry Secretary, Alan Johnson, a former union general secretary himself, retorted: 'Back ... [in the 1970s] this party supported secondary action and opposed the minimum wage. Now it's the other way round and that's how it needs to stay'.[69] So the Labour government ignored this protest.

Labour saw the strike question now as mainly settled and was silent on it in the election manifestos of 2001, 2005, 2010 and 2015. Ed Miliband, Labour Party leader (2010–15) in opposition, plumbed the depths when making public utterances to the effect that 'strikes are always a sign of failure'[70] – a far cry from Castle's acceptance of their inevitability. Yet the traditional view of Labour support for union freedoms had not been entirely extinguished in the parliamentary party and there have been two private members' bills on the subject in the recent past. Under Labour, backbencher John McDonnell presented an ambitious Trade Union Rights and Freedoms Bill in 2006, but there was no second reading and the Bill fell. In 2010, during the Coalition government, he presented a two-clause Lawful Industrial Action (Minor Errors) Bill; there was a second reading debate but the Bill was not pursued. Labour's 2017 general election manifesto, under Jeremy Corbyn's leadership, retained this minimalist approach by only calling for repeal of the 2016 Trade Union Act (which had doubled the strike notice to fourteen days, introduced high thresholds for strike ballots and put a time limit on a ballot's mandate).[71] This small step, though, had great symbolic importance.

In conclusion, for roughly its first 90 years the Labour Party was committed to upholding trade unions' freedom to strike. When in government, any measures restricting this were usually agreed with the TUC. This position broke down under the strain of the increasing weight of Tory legislation in the 1980s and Labour's third successive election defeat in 1987. By 1997, Labour (now "New Labour") had embraced the Tories' ultra-restrictive legislation almost totally. Ironically, Labour's conversion coincided with a rapid reduction in levels of strike activity, which had little to do with the changed legal environment and much to do with labour market weakness and employer hostility.

But New Labour in government was content to let the now much more limited number of strikes be sucked into the quagmire of post-1979 strike law – a world away from the five short sections of the 1906 TDA. Even under the simplicity of the latter, the Webbs could observe in 1920: 'It must not be imagined that either the ingenuity of

---

69 *Financial Times*, 27 and 28 September 2005.
70 *The Times*, 29 November 2011, the day before the largest-ever public service strike, which had seen over 2.5 million trade unionists balloted over pensions.
71 Labour Party, *For the Many Not the Few*, London, 2017.

the lawyers or the prejudice of the judges has been exhausted.'[72] Such words presciently fit the surreal nature of several court cases over the last twenty years, with judges sometimes taking the narrowest possible construction of the legislation while lawyers, at employers' behest, sniff out ever more fantastical grounds for court injunctions.[73] So can Labour, when next in government, reduce the intervention of the courts, start to restore trade unions' freedom to strike, and, in the process, return to one of its founding purposes?

---

72 S and B Webb, *History of Trade Unionism*, p.606.
73 See, for example, Keith Ewing, *Fighting Back: Resisting 'union-busting' and 'strike-breaking' in the BA dispute*, Liverpool, 2011.

Intellectuals and the Making of Labour Party Foreign Policy: The Forgotten Career of Leonard Woolf

David Morgan

"Historically, the Labour Party inherited its foreign policy from Cobden and Bright through Gladstonian liberalism," – Leonard Woolf.

Labour's distinctive brand of internationalism was shaped more by the liberal values of Bloomsbury than the theories of Marxism.

It is paradoxical that middle-class intellectuals were to be so central to the formulation of the foreign policy of Britain's main working-class party. Many of these intellectuals and writers were former Liberals drawn to the Labour Party as it emerged as a serious contender for government. This essay examines the long career of one the foremost party intellectuals: novelist, editor and journalist, Leonard Woolf, in order to understand the evolution of the party's internationalism over the first half of the last century.

"Leonard Woolf was one of the most prolific writers on international relations in Britain during the first half of the twentieth century," one observer, Peter Colin Wilson, concluded.[1] Woolf's contribution to the party's foreign policy was formidable as was his political career generally. He was a member of the Labour Party, the Fabian Society and the ILP. His intense political workload was to exasperate his wife, who remarked, 'politics go on all day, every day. L is entirely submerged. I might be a charwoman of the Prime Minister'.[2]

Leonard Woolf

Woolf's career as a Labour Party foreign policy theorist stretched from the First World War through to the onset of the Cold War and into the 1960s, but his greatest influence was during the interwar period. He worked closely with successive Labour leaders from Ramsay MacDonald to Harold Wilson. As well as sitting on strategically important policy committees, Woolf was a prolific

---

1 Peter Colin Wilson, *The International Theory of Leonard Woolf: An Exposition, Analysis and Assessment in the Light of his Reputation as a Utopian,* University of London thesis, 1997.
2 Virginia Woolf Letter to Ethel Smyth, 10 March 1936, *The Letters of Virginia Woolf 1936-1941,* ed Nigel Nicolson, Chatto & Windus, 1980.

writer on international affairs contributing to political journals such as *The Nation* and *New Statesman*.

Woolf's role has not always been fully appreciated. Towards the end of his life, Woolf estimated that he had spent some "200,000 hours" in exhaustive political work.[3] One of his most important books, *International Government*, influenced British government proposals for the League of Nations that were brought to the peace conference after the First World War.[4] Woolf was a tenacious advocate of the League of Nations and its successor, the United Nations, and believed strongly that a system of international arbitration was vital to save the world from future wars, which he saw as caused by secret diplomacy and lack of democratic control over foreign policy. Woolf was a key figure in the Union of Democratic Control, formed on 5 August 1914 just a day after Britain entered the First World War.[5]

Woolf's political output was immense, ambitious in scope and impressive in detail. His first foray into political research was on the cooperative movement, but it is as an expert on foreign policy and international relations that he excelled once he realised that it was the world situation that demanded his urgent attention. He understood that this was the main area where the labour movement needed expertise.

His research into the co-ops took him all over the country and the experience was to convert him into a lifelong supporter of co-operative ideals. Woolf produced three co-operative titles: *The Control of Industry by Co-operators and Trade Unionists* (1914); *Education and the Cooperative Movement* (1914); and *Co-operation and the War: Co-operative Action in National Crisis* (1915).

On the strength of his masterly research, Woolf was commissioned by the Webbs to undertake a study of professional associations in Britain for the Fabian Society. This led to a further invitation from Sidney Webb to study international agreements or "such international agreements as may prevent another war".[6] As a result, Woolf produced one of the earliest studies of international relations in his influential book, *International Government*, published in 1916. Today international relations theory is a thriving industry with its own university departments and plethora of think tanks, but in his day Woolf was breaking new ground.

Peter Colin Wilson states that, "The combination of overseas experience and critical acclaim for his books secured for him the position of Fabian 'expert' on international affairs, a status he retained throughout the inter-war period".[7]

---

3   Leonard Woolf, *Autobiography, Vol 2: 1911-1969*, Oxford University Press, 1980, p.480.
4   Ibid, p.481.
5   Duncan Wilson, *Leonard Woolf: A Political Biography*, The Hogarth Press, 1978, p.92.
6   Peter Colin Wilson, thesis.
7   Ibid.

Another of Woolf's publications, *Empire and Commerce in Africa,* established his reputation as a leading anti-imperialist theorist in Britain. Noticeable in his arguments on empire and colonialism, however, is a lack of reference to leading Marxist writers on imperialism such as Lenin and Rosa Luxemburg. This parochialism or insularity was a trait that Woolf shared with many Fabian and Labour theorists. It is identified as a significant weakness of labour intellectuals by John Saville.[8]

Woolf was to benefit from the reforms to Labour Party structure initiated by Arthur Henderson which culminated in the adoption of a new constitution in 1918. A main aim of the Henderson reforms was to transform the party into an efficient national, centrally organised body which would be an effective political machine. As part of these reforms the Advisory Committee on International Questions was set up to improve the party's mechanisms for developing foreign policy, whose function is explained by Rhiannon Vickers:

> *This body had responsibility for making recommendations to the Executive and the Parliamentary Party on foreign policy. Allied intervention in Russia was the first important issue that the committee discussed. At its first meeting of 30 May 1918, Sidney Webb was appointed chairman and Leonard Woolf secretary. Members included H N Brailsford, G D H Cole, Arnold Toynbee and, from July, Ramsay MacDonald.* [9]

Woolf remained secretary of this key policy committee from 1918 until 1945. In 1924, Ramsay MacDonald also made Woolf the secretary of the party's Advisory Committee on Imperial Questions and he continued in that post until 1945 as well. These offices and various other party roles gave Woolf "an important position within the Labour Party machine", says Duncan Wilson.[10] The new committees were not conceived simply as research bodies but were able to exert a direct influence on the party executive, its leadership and MPs. The international committee declared in an ambitious statement of aims that it saw itself as a "step in the direction of the much to be desired Democratisation of Foreign Policy".[11] It sought to act as a counterweight to the Foreign Office in the advice on government policy, says Wilson.

In Lucian Ashworth's opinion, "Woolf was a major influence on Labour's colonial policy and his views on the future of the empire became both Labour and British government policy after the war". [12]

---

8   John Saville, 'C R Attlee: An Assessment', *Socialist Register,* 1983.
9   Rhiannon Vickers, *The Labour Party and the World: The Evolution of Labour's Foreign Policy, 1900-1951, Volume One,* Manchester University Press, 2003, p.67.
10 Duncan Wilson, *Leonard Woolf,* p.126.
11 Ibid, p.128.
12 Lucian M Ashworth, *International Relations and the Labour Party: Intellectuals and Policy Making from 1918-1945,* Tauris Academic Studies, 2007, p.205.

Woolf's analysis could often be idiosyncratic. He was never satisfied with economic and materialist explanations of world problems; the influence of Freud's ideas, for instance, is evident in Woolf's concern for the psychological and cultural aspects.[13] He was to develop the notion of a "communal psychology" as a factor in political and international affairs.

He maintained an "abiding faith in the new liberalism that had emerged as a progressive alternative to the older laissez faire liberalism of the late 19th century".[14] This outlook necessarily shaped his understanding of capitalism whose failings for Woolf were that it "undermined the freedom of the embedded individual as well as sponsoring a capitalist class that could not be trusted to act in the interests of society as a whole".[15] It was an outlook that put him at odds with socialist colleagues who were influenced by Marxism. For Woolf, Cambridge philosopher G E Moore was his guide and this lifelong attachment to the liberal Moore's ideas often led him towards "intellectual sloppiness", according to Ashworth.[16]

But for years Woolf was to be strategically placed within the party structure as he worked to shape foreign policy and define the parameters of its internationalism. Woolf was extremely effective at filling the policy vacuum at a time when the bulk of party members were trade unionists far more preoccupied by economic struggles and social issues than the intricacies of foreign affairs. Although former trade unionist, Ernest Bevin, rose to become Labour's foreign secretary, most rank and file party activists would have found it difficult to acquire the expertise on foreign policy that Woolf had come to possess. Its origins and the overwhelmingly working-class composition of its membership compelled the party to rely on intellectuals to assist in the development of its policy. Woolf was to prove invaluable to party leaders as it evolved into a modern party of government. His work as policy committee secretary saw him "setting the agenda, drafting the minutes, and circulating papers and recommendations. In the inner circles of Labour policy-making, he was wanted on all sides as a facilitator and provider of information".[17]

Political Journalism

Apart from policy making and running a major publishing house, Woolf was a prolific political journalist who argued the case for international regulation, arbitration and peaceful settlement of disputes in the columns of several major journals and magazines read by people on the left. He helped to launch the *Political Quarterly,* serving as one of the journal's editors from 1931 to 1939. In addition, he held posts and contributed reviews, articles and opinion pieces to numerous journals

---

13 Ibid, p.205.
14 Ibid, p.126.
15 Ibid, p.126.
16 Ibid, p.125.
17 Victoria Glendinning, *Leonard Woolf: A Life,* Simon & Schuster, 2006, p.209.

and newspapers: Woolf was to be editor of the *Contemporary Review, The Nation* and *The New Statesman*, which is an impressive record of itself.

A Minor Figure?

Ben Pimlott's assessment of Woolf as "never more than a minor figure" in the party seems far from accurate or fair.[18] Woolf only once stood unsuccessfully for Parliament, he did not aspire to high office and adamantly refused honours, finding his forte in heading committees where policies were subjected to detailed scrutiny, debated and fashioned into concrete proposals that were brought to the attention of government ministers and party leaders. Committee work offered the ideal forum for Woolf to exercise his talents and he thrived as a researcher. As an advocate he was persuasive on a range of progressive causes which earned him a deserved reputation as a foreign policy expert.

It seems surprising that despite his extensive career in politics, Leonard Woolf is still mainly known for his marriage to Virginia and his association with the Bloomsbury Group. The son of a Jewish barrister, Woolf was well connected and, while at Cambridge, he formed important friendships that were to prove influential throughout his life. In 1902, he was invited to join the Cambridge Apostles whose recent members included Maynard Keynes, Lytton Strachey, Bertrand Russell and E M Forster. They espoused a radical liberalism that combined anti-imperialism, liberal social attitudes and a passionate opposition to war. During the First World War, several of this group became conscientious objectors and served time in gaol, although Woolf himself was declared medically unfit for military service.

Woolf came from a generation in revolt against the values of "bourgeois Victorianism" and who felt they were witnessing the beginning of a new era.[19] Woolf says that this revolt was started by writers such as Swinburne, Samuel Butler, Bernard Shaw, H G Wells and Thomas Hardy. Woolf and his peers regarded themselves as "passionately on the side of these champions of freedom of speech and freedom of thought, of common-sense and reason".

Woolf believed that he was involved in a "cosmic" struggle against "a religious and moral code of cant and hypocrisy which produced or condoned such social crimes and judicial murders as the condemnation of Dreyfus".[20]

---

18 Ben Pimlott, 'Was Anyone Afraid of Leonard Woolf?' *New Society*, 5 October 1978, in *Frustrate Their Knavish Tricks: Writings on Biography, History and Politics*, Harper Collins, 1994.
19 L Woolf, *Autobiography, Vol 1*, OUP, p.96.
20 Ibid, p.96.

Dreyfus

Woolf regarded the vindication of Dreyfus as a possible "turning point in European history and civilisation".[21] The case was significant for Woolf in several respects, not least in the role of the writer Emile Zola whose courageous intervention in the affair offered an inspiring lesson about the potential power that could be wielded by the writer's pen. Through Zola's example, as Woolf acknowledged, he was able to realise how one solitary intellectual could help right injustice and eventually transform public opinion.[22] Zola became a role model in his passion for truth and deep hatred of injustice and how he was fully prepared to incur the wrath of the law, the mob and the conservative establishment.[23] In his famous article, *J'accuse!*, Zola issued a cry of rage against the treatment of Colonel Dreyfus and appealed to the republican and humanitarian values of justice, liberty, brotherhood, science, humanity and progress; exactly those values that inspired the young and idealistic Woolf.

Zola's role in the Dreyfus Affair had attracted the attention of the British left and the issues it raised were, for example, discussed by the Fabians in 1890 in a talk by Sidney Olivier on "Emile Zola as Artist and as Doctrinaire", which addressed Zola's revolt against injustice.[24] In the same Fabian programme, Shaw was to speak about Ibsen. In the literary press "Zolaism" had become an abusive term for novelists who dared to write about sexual matters.[25]

Education

Woolf was a scholarship boy from an impoverished middle-class background whose father died when he was still a child. Young Leonard underwent a typical mandarin education at St Paul's School, London, before ending up at Trinity College, Cambridge.[26] His schooling, in Latin and Greek classics, "affected the cast of his mind".[27]

Woolf grew up with "a sense of standing apart" from the mainstream after having completely abandoned religion at the age of fourteen.[28] He demonstrated "little apparent consciousness" of being Jewish. His militant atheism put a distance between him and many activists in the labour movement.

From the evidence of his school essays, his early political outlook was very conventional indeed. In one essay on Disarmament and Civilisation, Woolf argued

---

21 Ibid, p.97.
22 L Woolf, *Vol 2*, p.391.
23 Philip Walker, *Zola*, RKP, 1985, p.227.
24 Michael Rosen, *The Disappearance of Emile Zola: Love, Literature and the Dreyfus Case*, Faber, 2017, p.173.
25 Ibid, p.179.
26 Duncan Wilson, *Leonard Woolf*, p.12.
27 Ibid, p.27.
28 Ibid, p.12.

that disarming was dangerous because Europe needed a deterrent "against the Yellow Peril".[29]

The Apostles

It was the Apostles that did most for shaping Woolf's intellectual formation, according to Duncan Wilson.[30] The Apostles or Cambridge Conversazione Society, first founded in 1820 at Cambridge University, have been the subject of much lurid speculation concerning alleged promotion of homosexuality and infiltration by Communists, particularly in the light of the exposure of the so-called "Cambridge spies", of whom only two, Guy Burgess and Anthony Blunt, were ever actual members of the Apostles.[31]

As an exclusive, self-perpetuating social organisation, the Apostles provided those who were fortunate to be invited into membership with a highly privileged network of contacts to the upper echelons of society on whom they were able to draw for the rest of their lives. It was a semi-secret, all-male body that gave access to people of influence across various professions and in government. Membership opened many doors to which non-members, no matter how talented, could never hope to aspire. Bertrand Russell held that the sense of belonging fostered by the society was a good preparation for a role in running the world.[32] Woolf described the Apostles as the "greatest happiness" of his time at Cambridge.[33]

Eric Hobsbawm, himself an Apostle, saw his own invitation, as one "that hardly any Cambridge undergraduate was likely to refuse, since even revolutionaries like to be in a suitable tradition" and expressed his pride in being associated with the illustrious members of the past.[34] These "absolutely admirable" qualities that Hobsbawm identifies with the Apostles were lasting friendship and intellectual honesty.[35]

Woolf obviously made use of the opportunities that it brought him as he embarked on his political, publishing and journalistic careers. Woolf rarely questioned his entitlement to be a part of this privileged minority. For example, he was fully prepared to make use of his old Cambridge connections to find a job for his nephew, Julian Bell, with the Labour politician, Hugh Dalton.[36]

The society exerted a specific influence in literary London where, "Apostles were regular contributors to the book review pages of many papers and magazines",

---

29 Ibid, p.14.
30 Ibid, p30.
31 Richard Deacon, *The Cambridge Apostles: A History of Cambridge University's elite intellectual secret society*, Robert Royce Limited, 1985, p47.
32 Ronald W Clark, *The Life of Bertrand Russell*, Weidenfeld and Nicolson; 1975, p42.
33 L Woolf, Vol 1, p68.
34 Eric Hobsbawm, *Interesting Times: A Twentieth Century Life*, Abacus, 2006, p.188.
35 Ibid, p.190.
36 *Letters of Leonard Woolf* ed Frederic Spotts, Bloomsbury, 1990, p.576.

Richard Deacon asserts, pointing out that Desmond MacCarthy was in control of the literary pages of the *New Statesman*, Lytton Strachey's uncle was at the helm of *The Spectator* while Leonard Woolf was in charge of *The Nation*.[37] Many of the authors published by the Woolfs' Hogarth Press were Apostles.

It has been argued that during the interwar years, several Apostles, although never a formal advocacy group, exerted considerable influence on Britain's foreign policy and expressed similar views on the First World War, the League of Nations, the British Empire and international trade.[38]

Bloomsbury

To a large extent the Bloomsbury Group was an extension of the Cambridge Apostles in London – but with the addition of women participants. Virginia Woolf stated that the very thought of the all-male Cambridge atmosphere made her "vomit...green vomit".[39] Summing up Bloomsbury, Quentin Bell identifies its anti-establishment attitude as a defining feature: "Bloomsbury was always in some degree at war with the establishment, and from an early date made it clear that nothing, or at any rate very little, was to be sacred".[40]

Nevertheless, the coterie's perceived elitism could provoke extreme reactions. It is difficult to disentangle Bloomsbury's infamous dispute with novelist D H Lawrence, from the deep social chasm between this miner's son and the socially privileged Bloomsbury. Lawrence's fear that he would be "intimidated" was deeply visceral, telling fellow author, David Garnett, who had made the initial introductions, that, "I feel I should go mad when I think of your set, Duncan Grant and Keynes and (Francis) Birrell. It makes me dream of beetles. In Cambridge I had a similar dream".[41]

Literary critic, F R Leavis, a champion of Lawrence, later used the incident to denounce the whole "Cambridge-Bloomsbury milieu".[42] The irreverence and scepticism associated with the Bloomsbury outlook were vital aspects of Woolf's writing. The attitude is more typically associated with Lytton Strachey whose, *Eminent Victorians*, published in 1918, captured the post-war mood of disenchantment with tarnished heroes. It is a book described by Quentin Bell as "a

37 Deacon, p.79.
38 Daniela Donnini Macciò, *Ethics, economics and power in the Cambridge Apostles' internationalism between the two world wars*, European Journal of International Relations, 2015.
39 Virginia Woolf, when thinking of Cambridge, would "vomit [...] a green vomit which gets into the ink and blisters the paper", Letter to Lytton Strachey, cited by Ingrid Carson, *A Bid for Freedom: Talking Back in Virginia Woolf's Orlando*, University of North Carolina, 2007.
40 Quentin Bell, *Bloomsbury*, p.78.
41 Ibid, p.71.
42 Ibid, p.73.

tract for the times". But what Leonard Woolf valued of Bloomsbury was the persistent necessity of "questioning the truth and utility of everything".[43]

Raymond Williams acutely conveys the ideological nature of Bloomsbury; in his essay, "The Bloomsbury Fraction", he characterises it as part of a "minority culture" and "intellectual aristocracy".[44] Interestingly, Quentin Bell describes the 'Bloomsberries' as an actual aristocracy, noting that, "a large element of Bloomsbury was composed of the heirs of 'aristocratic' families".[45] Williams, still seeking to praise the social conscience that was a "typical characteristic of the group", commends their "remarkable record of political and organisational involvement".[46] Leonard Woolf stands as an example of this milieu and, alongside Bertrand Russell as peace activist and Maynard Keynes as reforming economist, he was to exert most influence in 20th century British politics. But a key point that Raymond Williams makes is that Bloomsbury should be located in the social hierarchy as a "civilising fraction of their class".[47]

Colonial Administrator

On leaving Cambridge, Woolf needed to earn a living and opted to join the colonial civil service where he served in Ceylon for seven years. It was not his first career choice but the experience was to prove a formative one for the growth of his political awareness and the strengthened of his opposition to imperialism. Woolf's views provoked Beatrice Webb to speak of him as "an anti-imperialist fanatic but otherwise a moderate in Labour politics, always an opponent of workers' control and proletarianism".[48]

On his return to England, Woolf wrote his first of two novels, *The Village in the Jungle*, based on his life in Ceylon, married Virginia Stephen, who quipped about marrying a "penniless Jew", and took up his work as a political theorist, researcher, policy maker, journalist and editor, beginning a career of more than fifty years.[49]

In 1917 he and Virginia founded the Hogarth Press which expanded into a successful publisher of a wide range of titles including political works by established authors such as J M Keynes, H G Wells and J A Hobson. Hogarth also pioneered the translation of Russian literature into English and the Woolfs even learned Russian to help with the translation and editing. The press was the first to publish the collected works of Sigmund Freud in the English language, translated by an Apostle friend, James Strachey. Freudian psychoanalysis was to influence Woolf's later political

43 Ibid, p.80.
44 Raymond Williams, *The Bloomsbury Fraction*, in *Problems in Materialism and Culture*, Verso, 1980, p.150.
45 Bell, *Bloomsbury*, p.85.
46 Williams, *Bloomsbury Fraction*, p.155.
47 Ibid, p.169.
48 *The Diaries of Beatrice Webb*, ed Norman and Jean MacKenzie, Virago, 2000, p.458.
49 Quentin Bell, *Virginia Woolf, Vol 2*, p.2.

writings, in particular *After the Deluge* and *Principia Politica*, which are each subtitled, "a study in communal psychology".

Into Politics

The Russian Revolution of 1917 was a key world event that shaped Woolf's emerging political consciousness. As he states in his autobiography, it was the First World War and the revolutions in Russia that drew him into active politics:

> As the war went on, I became more and more entangled in politics. The Russian revolution of 1917 was a tremendous event for me and for all those whose beliefs and hopes had been moulded in the revolutionary fires of liberty, equality and fraternity.[50]

Explaining his life in politics, the bulk of which he describes as "dreary work" on committees, Woolf states that he could not remain satisfied with "acquiescent resignation" in the face of impending disaster. His "first contact with the economic system of capitalism in England" was in 1912 when he briefly worked for a charity dealing with poverty in the slums of Hoxton.[51] This brief episode was followed by his work on co-operative societies where he says that witnessing the "lives of working class co-operators in the north confirmed my socialism". The "senseless war" completed his conversion to political activism.

International Government

Woolf soon emerged as "the main foreign policy expert in the Fabian Research Bureau"[52] and within the Labour Party, but he frequently expressed doubts about his own commitment and often adopted a self-deprecating tone when writing to close friends like Lytton Strachey:

> I have been absolutely submerged in internationalism. The result will I imagine be the lowest pit of dullness. It would make it easier if I knew something about history.[53]

In his autobiography he surveys over five decades of painstaking policy advocacy and methodical political work only to conclude that he had "achieved practically nothing", forlornly commenting that:

> The world today and the history of the human anthill during the last fifty-seven years would be exactly the same as it is if I had played ping pong instead of sitting on committees and writing books and memoranda.[54]

---

50 L Woolf, Vol 2, p.150.
51 Ibid, p.477.
52 Ashworth, *International Relations*, p.204.
53 Woolf to Lytton Strachey, 8 February 1915, *Woolf Letters*, p.385.
54 L Woolf, *Vol 2*, p.480.

Despite this "failure", and apparent despair, Woolf always believed that doing nothing was never a serious option. Consequently, his comments about being ineffective should not be taken too seriously. His record speaks for itself; he never ceased trying to persuade political leaders to adopt his proposals to end conflict and achieve greater social justice in the world.

He gave specific attention to the British Empire, especially India and Africa, recognising that these were countries where Labour in government could make a real difference. Woolf claims some credit for the policy that the 1945 Attlee administration adopted towards granting India its freedom, although he believed that it could have been achieved without the violence and loss of life had previous governments implemented his proposals much earlier.[55]

"Like the leading Fabians, he saw government as a regulatory activity. International government therefore meant international regulation," John Callaghan states.[56]

"Woolf assumed that the evolution of international organisation was destined to supplant rather than coexist with power politics and the balance of power system, but he offered no evidence for this optimism," concludes Callaghan in a major study of Labour foreign policy.

Woolf generally argued that governments needed to take enlightened reforms as an essential means of averting revolt from below. His attitude was strongly based in his class background and his most frightening experiences as a child, he recalled, were when he encountered London's slum dwellers. The brooding, "murmur" of the crowd was his worst fear.[57]

Fabianism

The Fabian Society became the natural home for progressive-minded intellectuals like Woolf. They were a group described by Eric Hobsbawm as "the only British socialist body to appeal to intellectuals" and as "resolutely non-proletarian".[58] Hobsbawm stresses that before the First World War, the policies of the Fabians were "always at variance with those of most other sections of the political left". However, the Labour Party depended on the Fabians like Woolf for policy ideas, especially concerning its support for international institutions such as the League of Nations and its position on the decolonisation of the British Empire after 1945.

In its preoccupation with domestic social reforms and national economic policies, the labour movement often neglected international affairs and its thinkers ignored

55 Ibid, p.353.
56 John Callaghan, *The Labour Party and Foreign Policy: A History*, Routledge, 2007, p.34.
57 L Woolf, *Autobiography, Vol 1*, p.43.
58 Eric Hobsbawm, *The Fabians Reconsidered*, in *Labouring Men*, p.256.

how foreign policy could impact on the domestic situation. This is a weakness still in evidence in the 1950s when the *New Fabian Essays* appeared ushering in the new thinking of contributors such as Anthony Crosland. Only one of these essays addressed foreign policy. As John Saville put it, "What the New Fabian Essayists in general missed was the central importance of foreign policies and politics to domestic affairs in Britain during the years of war and its aftermath".[59]

Russia and Revolution

Woolf's attitude to Russia was complex and evolved over time. He would certainly never have become a Communist and didn't really grasp Marxism, but initially he enthusiastically welcomed the Russian revolution as a step towards greater human freedom. He would continue to see the February revolution as "essential for the future of European civilisation".[60]

Woolf was one of the 1,150 delegates to the "Great Labour, Socialist and Democratic Convention" held in Leeds on 3 June 1917. This gathering was perhaps the most remarkable expression of anti-war and pro-revolutionary sentiment that the British labour movement has ever witnessed. The Convention praised the Russian Revolution as an inspiration, voted to defend civil liberties, called for an end to the war and pledged to set up Workers' and Soldiers' Councils in Britain in solidarity with the Soviets that were being formed in Russia.

The Convention heard impassioned speeches from prominent Labour and socialist activists including Bertrand Russell, Ramsay MacDonald, Sylvia Pankhurst, Tom Mann, Philip Snowden, Charlotte Despard, Ernest Bevin, Dora Montefiore and Willie Gallacher. Woolf later described the event as "one of the most enthusiastic and emotional" that he had ever attended. Russell was keen to stress that the convention was an expression of solidarity with the "Kerensky revolution".[61]

Woolf, quickly disillusioned with Russia once the Bolsheviks consolidated their power, by April 1920 could be found writing:

> *I hope you don't think I'm anti-Bolshevik. I'm not. I think they're the only people who've made an honest and serious attempt to practice what I believe in. But I can't help seeing their faults and mistakes which, if persisted in, will undo the good they've done.*[62]

He was nevertheless staunchly opposed to the Allied intervention in 1918 after Russia's withdrawal from the war, although in private remarks he risked sounding like an adolescent schoolboy:

---

59 John Saville, *CR Attlee: An Assessment*, Socialist Register, 1983.
60 Glendinning, *Leonard Woolf*, p.210.
61 Bertrand Russell, *Autobiography, Vol 2: 1914-1944*, Allen and Unwin, 1968, p.31.
62 L Woolf, *Letters*, p.389.

The Russian intervention is far the most beastly thing which has happened in the war. For us to start killing Russians merely because they wont fight is really the limit.[63]

The 1917 Club

Woolf founded the 1917 Club to discuss the Russian Revolution. According to Quentin Bell, "Bloomsbury formed an important element of the 1917 Club".[64]

The club's first meeting in December 1917 attracted many notable political and literary figures. It was where Woolf first got to know Ramsay MacDonald well; like many and with good reason he didn't trust him. Woolf says that the majority of the club's members were in the Labour Party, but it also drew in unaffiliated radicals and independent-minded liberals. There was an overlap with Bloomsbury figures and those who joined other London debating societies such as the Rainbow Circle, a largely Liberal Party think tank, although Fabians and MacDonald were involved in that too.[65]

Members of the 1917 Club, whose premises were at 4 Gerrard Street, Soho, included figures such as G D H Cole, C E M Joad, Francis Meynell, Raymond Postgate, H N Brailsford and Stanley Unwin. At least one Communist, Emile Burns, was involved.[66]

It was Brailsford who was to produce one of the early studies of the new Soviet system in his book, *How the Soviets Work*, written between 1920 and 1927. Brailsford wrote from an ethical socialist perspective sympathetic to the new workers' state, although he was keen to point out that the pioneers of the Russian revolutionary struggle were not Communists, but the Narodniks, whom, he says, were "almost exclusively intellectuals…and they included several men and women who were aristocrats by birth".[67] While challenging some of the methods of the Bolsheviks, Brailsford concluded that through its survival of the years of blockade and civil war "it has won its right to understanding and respect. But, above all, it has won its right to peace". It was a position that Woolf broadly shared.

The importance of the Russian revolution in shaping Labour Party policy has often been underestimated. Since the time of the forged Zinoviev letter scandal Labour has felt compelled to define its own brand of socialism in opposition to Bolshevik Russia and Soviet "state socialism". In foreign policy terms, the party hierarchy was determined never to be seen as "soft on Moscow". Woolf was neither able nor willing

---

63 Ibid, p.222.
64 Bell, *Bloomsbury*, p.68.
65 *Minutes of the Rainbow Circle, 1894-1924*, ed Michael Freeden, Camden 4th Series, Royal Historical Society, UCL, 1989.
66 Woolf, *Vol 2*, p.156.
67 H N Brailsford, *How the Soviets Work*, Vanguard Press, November 1927.

to set out a persuasive alternative to this position which became virulently anti-Communist during the Cold War.

Class

Although active in Labour politics, Woolf seems to have found it difficult to disguise his strong class prejudices. As Ben Pimlott wrote, Woolf's closest friendships were with people who were "snobbishly disdainful of the working class"[68] and Woolf never entirely escaped from such class snobbery. According to Claud Cockburn, Woolf was "so English" that he was "a vividly stimulating caricature of his own nationality".[69] He was an unusual kind of socialist.

In 1917 Woolf visited the industrial north for a series of speaking engagements at the invitation of the Women's Cooperative Society during which he lodged with families of local activists. He was there to argue the case for international government, an increasingly popular cause after three years of war. It was a rare experience for him to meet the working class and see how they lived.

Woolf's remarks in letters to his wife betray the attitudes of his class towards the "lower orders" whom he would usually only meet as domestic servants or menial workers.

Writing from Manchester on 30 November 1917, Woolf informs Virginia of the people he had met and describes the homes where he was lodging. His comments on their lack of intelligence and uncleanliness are as offensive as references to cabbage smells and flies on the food that George Orwell claimed to see in workers' homes and lodging houses. Contrast this with Engels, who remarked that the "bourgeois was perfectly justified in his fears" but welcomed the workers' growing restlessness.[70]

One woman activist whom Woolf met was "of the ultra-pacifist type and full of good conversation culled from Morel, Bertie (Russell) and Goldie (Dickinson) and watered by a dim understanding."

In the same letter he describes the person chairing his lecture as "horrid (literally) and dirty" and describes his lecture as too difficult for his audience: "They asked many questions but it was a little too difficult for them".[71]

Others he met are described as comic characters, such as Mrs Eckhard of Didsbury, who "dates most things in her life from the day on which she had her appendix removed",[72] a creation worthy of playwright Alan Bennett, but surely incongruous to hear spoken by a leading socialist.

---

68 Pimlott, *Writings*, p.63.
69 Patricia Cockburn, *The Years of the Week*, Penguin, 1971, p.25.
70 Frederick Engels, *The Condition of the Working Class in England*, Granada Publishing, 1982, introduced by Eric Hobsbawm, p.152.
71 L Woolf, *Letters*, p.216.
72 Ibid, p.218.

Africa and Empire

Empire and Commerce in Africa published in 1920 is seen as "an important landmark in Woolf's thinking and writing about imperialism".[73] In the book, initially commissioned by the Fabians, Woolf mainly focuses on Abyssinia and the British annexation of Uganda in an analysis that clearly owes a debt to J A Hobson. Through use of up-to-date official statistics, Woolf proves that empire at least in the short term did not pay. He harshly criticises the misplaced assumptions of pro-imperialists that British rule was a good thing for the African people.[74] He employed the piercing irony of Lytton Strachey to expose the follies of British empire builders, describing one leading official as, "one of those fortunate persons whose early life was chiefly occupied in killing things".[75]

However, Woolf was no advocate of immediate independence for Africa; in fact, he argued that withdrawal would simply leave the territories vulnerable to "more cruel exploitation by irresponsible white men".[76] In expressing such opinions, Woolf was very much of his time. He concluded that the existing colonial powers could be transformed into trustees rather than exploiters of the native populations, which today seems a naïve point of view.

In describing the motivations of states and peoples Woolf resorted to the argument that a "communal psychology" was the overriding determining factor in foreign and imperial policy. This exposes a central weakness in his general approach which can be traced back to his adoption of the reasoning of his mentor, G E Moore.

Notwithstanding its political weaknesses, the book made a tremendous impact on political opinion. As Philip Noel Baker stated, "it stirred the conscience of the Colonial Powers, and evoked the sense of trusteeship for subject peoples".[77]

Woolf and Cambridge philosopher G E Moore

73 Duncan Wilson, *Leonard Woolf*, p.113.
74 Ibid, p.114.
75 Ibid, p.115.
76 Ibid, p.117.
77 George Spater and Ian Parsons, *A Marriage of Two Minds: An Intimate Portrait of Leonard and Virginia Woolf*, Cape/Hogarth Press, 1977, p.94.

It has been suggested that the book was a collaborative effort by Leonard and Virginia following the discovery of nearly 800 pages of notes that had been taken by Virginia Woolf as background research for the study.[78]

Woolf's concern for the plight of Africa and preoccupation with colonial issues are further reflected in books published by the Hogarth Press in the 1930s, when it became "a key disseminator of fiction by colonial writers as well as a notable publication route for anti-imperialist thought".[79] Titles in its Day to Day political pamphlets series included CLR James, *The Case for West Indian Self-Government* (1933); WG Ballinger, *Race and Economics in South Africa* (1934); Leonard Woolf, *The League and Abyssinia* (1936); Leonard Barnes, *The Future of the Colonies* (1936) among others. Hogarth also pioneered the publication in English of new African literature such as Kenyan writer Githendu Parmenas Mockerie's *An African Speaks for His People* (1934). Hogarth thus made a notable contribution to the dissemination of anti-imperialist ideas in Britain.

A Utopian?

To dismiss Woolf's ideas as hopelessly utopian is to ignore his major influence on Labour policy. Peter Colin Wilson identifies as utopianism Woolf's unwavering support for the League of Nations and his belief in human progress through the exercise of reason.[80]

Ultimately Woolf's approach to politics derives from the philosophy of G E Moore, the leading thinker in the Cambridge Apostles. Woolf compared Moore's "simple" nature to Dostoyevsky's Prince Myshkin.

Moore's biographer, Paul Levy, comments that Woolf "applied Moore's method of defining duty to an historical and political purpose.[81] Woolf "regarded himself as a member of Moore's inner circle", and the philosopher was to be a lifelong inspiration.[82] When Woolf was once asked by Beatrice Webb if he had ever met a truly great man, he simply replied with the name, "Moore".[83]

Moore's main work, *Principia Ethica*, first published in 1903, is often seen as the bible of Bloomsbury. The book was described by Moore's fellow Apostle, Bertrand Russell, as "a triumph of lucidity". The chapter that most influenced Woolf's outlook is the one titled, "Ethics in Relation to Conduct", according to Levy.[84]

---

78 Anna Snaith, *Leonard and Virginia Woolf: writing against empire*, King's College London, 2013.
79 Ibid.
80 Peter Colin Wilson, thesis.
81 Paul Levy, *Moore: G E Moore and the Cambridge Apostles*, Oxford, 1981, p.239.
82 Ibid, p.236.
83 Duncan Wilson, *Leonard Woolf* p.19.
84 Levy, *Moore*, p.239.

Moore examines propositions such as "what is good in itself?", "what conduct is a means to good results?", "what ought we to do?", "What actions are right?" and what is a person's real duty. These questions were urgent ones for any idealistic person contemplating his or her future career and seeking to make a mark in public life, as Woolf was intent on doing. In fact, Woolf's entire political career is a lifelong pursuit of Moore's liberal ideals.

Moore's method of reasoning that was so influential on Woolf had both its strengths and weaknesses. Moore urged a critical approach to established social and intellectual conventions, but his searching for simple solutions brought with it "the implied conviction that there were simple if often unexpected answers", Duncan Wilson argues. "This search for the simple questions was to be a feature of Woolf's political attitudes, sometimes a strength and sometimes a weakness".[85]

Woolf's simplification of complex political issues is evident in his response to the rise of fascism and to Soviet Russia, topics which are controversially addressed in his book, *Barbarians at the Gate,* which brought Woolf into conflict with Victor Gollancz and the Left Book Club. In this book, Woolf argued that the world had entered into a struggle between the forces of "barbarism and civilisation", drawing little distinction between the fascist and Communist variants of "authoritarianism". As Duncan Wilson says dryly, Moore did not "always protect him from simplifying political problems".[86]

In the 1940s, Woolf wrote extensively on the challenges of post-war reconstruction, but was again chided for offering simplistic solutions to grand and intractable problems. Woolf believed that the law and proper regulation offered the main protection against civilisation's descent into anarchy and barbarism. Predatory capitalism had to be controlled.[87]

Peter Colin Wilson is critical of Woolf's "highly simplistic manner", citing his comparison of world government with the running of a football club: "There is nothing essentially different in the government of a football club, a village, a town, a country, of Europe, or of the world, except that the scale is bigger and the organisation more complicated".[88]

Into the Cold War

Woolf's final major contribution to Labour's policy debate was a Fabian pamphlet published in November 1947, *Foreign Policy: The Labour Party's Dilemma,* which appeared on the cusp of the Cold War. Its origins lay in the aim of the Fabian International Committee to define the broad framework of a "socialist foreign policy"

---

85 Duncan Wilson, *Leonard Woolf,* p.27.
86 Ibid, p.28.
87 Ashworth, *International Relations,* p.208.
88 Peter Colin Wilson, thesis.

for the new Attlee government. At the time Labour politicians were debating whether to retain a favourable approach to the Soviet Union or to join wholeheartedly in the emerging Atlantic alliance of capitalist powers headed by the United States formed to confront the USSR.

Woolf begins with the premise that the most urgent matter is to prevent the outbreak of another war and he believed the mutual suspicions between the US and the USSR posed inherent dangers for Britain and the world. An independent foreign policy, he argues, would entail a refusal to become entangled in global power politics and to refrain from taking sides in the US-USSR hostilities.

While Woolf believed that total isolationism was economically impracticable, he concluded that Britain could still operate with a fair degree of independence. He concluded that what was needed wasn't neutrality as such, but impartiality which would see the UK occasionally siding with the US and at other times siding with the USSR, depending on the country's national interests.

Woolf urged the post-war Labour government not to begin preparations for a future war and to retain only sufficient armed forces required to deter aggression.

On the formation of the post-war Atlantic alliance, rearmament and atomic weapons, Woolf's proposals were not to find favour with Attlee's Labour Party. Neither did Woolf's independent policy meet with the approval of the left. MP Konni Zilliacus, for example, dismissed Woolf's pamphlet as little more than an example of what he called the "Churchill-Truman-Attlee-Bevin hysteria about Communism".[89]

Contrary to Woolf's long held demand for greater openness in diplomacy, the Attlee government was to conduct business with Washington in an unprecedented degree of secrecy, as Saville outlines. Under Attlee "Britain became a willing accomplice in the expansion of the US armed presence in Europe primed to launch action against the Soviet Union". The country was turned into a site for a vast network of American bases and decisions on their location were "taken almost wholly in secret".[90] Major decisions of defence and foreign policy were also taken "...in secret not only from the public, but from Parliament, and in quite a number of quite central matters, from a majority of Cabinets."

When he wrote *The Labour Party in Perspective* in 1937 Attlee had argued that a socialist foreign policy would look very different from a Tory one, but he had radically changed his view by the time the war ended to a belief that "parties should be united in defence and foreign policy", according to Attlee's recent biographer Michael Jago.[91]

---

89   Duncan Wilson, *Leonard Woolf*, p.213.
90   Saville, 'C R Attlee', p.33.
91   Michael Jago, *Clement Attlee: The Inevitable Prime Minister*, 2017, p.184.

Once in office Attlee and Bevin proceeded to adopt a bipartisan approach particularly towards the USSR. By 1946, "Attlee, Bevin and the Chiefs of Staff were unanimous in their conviction that the Soviet Union would push at any weak spot that appeared and that this must be resisted at all costs".[92] Thus the Cold War was born under a Labour government and Woolf ideas didn't seem to matter too much.

Similarly, Woolf's call for a renunciation of the Atomic bomb fell on deaf ears. He would not have been aware of the secret negotiations taking place between Attlee and the Americans. On this Attlee's policy was as secretive as that of Churchill, Saville argues.[93] There was an absence of serious discussion about the bomb at full Cabinet where atomic energy and its implications rarely made the agenda. A small select committee took all major decisions.

Conclusion

While Woolf remained consistently on the left politically, he was often well out of step with the dominant political mood and was reluctant to join any factions. His independence of mind is certainly a positive feature of his writings, but at the same time he held firm to certain personal shibboleths and often enunciated social prejudices peculiar for a socialist.

Ben Pimlott applauds Woolf's efforts to change Labour policy and widen its vision to encompass the colonial peoples struggling for their independence and is probably correct to maintain that "Labour's modest record of support for colonial movements owes much to the work of Woolf"; in addition Pimlott argues that "Labour's approach to foreign affairs would have been less confident, less practical, less open-minded without him".[94] If this is only partly an accurate assessment, then Woolf's achievements are worthy of note.

Furthermore, in *International Government*, Woolf had produced "one of the seminal publications which can be said to have guided the creators of the League of Nations".[95]

His advocacy of a world citizenship is alone a cause worth fighting for. When he was arguing this position in the early 20th century he was very much a minority voice. Few people felt or thought internationally, as John Callaghan points out, and the popular feeling is perhaps not so dissimilar one hundred years later.[96]

While Leonard Woolf's thought might often appear to be little more than wishful thinking and his reasoning prone to be simplistic, his arguments for democratic

---

92 Ibid, p.187.
93 John Saville, *The Price of Alliance: American Bases in Britain*, Socialist Register, 1987, p.37.
94 Pimlott, *Writings*, p.66.
95 Callaghan, *Labour Party and Foreign Policy*, p.34.
96 Ibid, p.35.

regulation of international affairs cannot be too easily dismissed especially by those who really want to see a world with less conflict and war.

His tenacity, staying power and enduring commitment are admirable qualities even if sometimes his ideas were often wrongheaded and outdated. Woolf stood for some fundamental values and perennial truths such as the urgent need for negotiated settlements to avoid wars that could have catastrophic consequences. For all his faults, Woolf was on the side of the "angels"[97] and his contributions to Labour Party's internationalism can still be profitably scrutinised; he has possibly still got much to say about an independent foreign policy for Labour.

Labour poster 1957

---

97 "Angels" was the term for Apostles who had left Cambridge after graduating and "taken wing" into the world.

Notes on Contributors

John Belchem

John Belchem's interest in the history of radicalism dates to his undergraduate student days at the University of Sussex some fifty years ago where he was subsequently supervised by Asa Briggs and J F C Harrison. He is now Emeritus Professor of History at the University of Liverpool and Chair of the Society for the Study of Labour History.

Duncan Bowie

Duncan Bowie is a senior research associate at UCL. He is the author of *The Radical and Socialist Tradition in British Planning* (Routledge, 2018); *Roots of the British Socialist Movement* (SHS, 2014) and two books on housing and planning policy. Duncan's latest book, *Revolt and Reform in the City of Dreaming Spires* will be published by the University of Westminster Press in November 2018. He is a member of the SHS committee and since 2005 he has written a history column for Chartist magazine, of which he is reviews editor.

Keith Laybourn

Keith Laybourn is Diamond Jubilee Professor of the University of Huddersfield. He is the author and editor of many books on labour history, women and unemployment, philanthropy, working-class gambling, and policing in Britain during the inter-war years. A recent book is *Marxism in Britain: Dissent, Decline and Re-emergence 1945-c.2000* (Routledge, 2015). Keith recently edited and contributed to, *Labour and Working Class Lives* (MUP,2017) and *Secular Martyrdom: From Peterloo to the Present* (Routledge, 2018). Keith is President of the Society for the Study of Labour History.

Dave Lyddon

Dr Dave Lyddon was, until retirement, senior lecturer in industrial relations at Keele University. He is co-author of *Glorious Summer: Class Struggle in Britain 1972* (2001) and co-editor of *Strikes around the World* (2007). Dave was founding editor of *Historical Studies in Industrial Relations* and is the treasurer of the Society for the Study of Labour History.

David Morgan

David is a journalist, editor and speech writer. He writes essays, polemics, reviews and poetry. He edited and contributed an article on Freudian Psychoanalysis and Revolution to *1917, The Russian Revolution, Reactions and Impact,* (SHS, 2017). David was co-editor of the book, *A Permanent State of Terror?* (London, 2003). He is Secretary of the Socialist History Society.

Graham Taylor

Graham Taylor has written extensively on the history of the labour movement. In 1978 he published, with Jack Dromey, an account of the Grunwick Strike, *Grunwick: The Workers' Story,* (second edition, 2016). Recently, after retiring as a history lecturer, Graham published *Ada Salter: Pioneer of Ethical Socialism* (2016). He is a member of the Socialist History Society.

Willie Thompson

Willie Thompson was, until his retirement, professor of contemporary history at Glasgow Caledonian University. He is a former secretary of the SHS and former editor of our journal, *Socialist History*. His books include *The Good Old Cause: British Communism 1920-1991, What Happened to History?,* and *Ideologies in the Age of Extremes: Liberalism, Conservatism, Communism, Fascism 1914-91.* His most recent book was *Work, Sex and Power: The forces that shaped our history,* (2015).

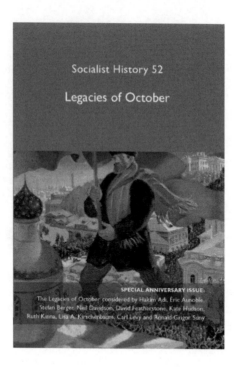

Socialist History 52

Legacies of October

SPECIAL ANNIVERSARY ISSUE:
The Legacies of October considered by Hakim Adi, Eric Aunoble,
Stefan Berger, Neil Davidson, David Featherstone, Kate Hudson,
Ruth Kinna, Lisa A. Kirschenbaum, Carl Levy and Ronald Grigor Suny

The Socialist History Society

The Socialist History Society was founded in 1992 and includes many leading Socialist and labour historians, academic and amateur researchers, in Britain and overseas. The SHS holds regular events, public meeting controversies. We produce a range of publications, including the journal Socialist History and a regular Newsletter.

The SHS is the successor to the Communist Party History Group, which was established in 1946 and is now totally independent of all political parties and groups. We are engaged in and seek to encourage historical studies from a Marxist and broadly-defined left perspective. We are interested in all aspects of human history from the earliest social formations to the present day and aim for an international approach.

We are particularly interested in the various struggles of labour, of women, of progressive campaigns and peace movements around the world, as well as the history of colonial peoples, black people, and all oppressed communities seeking justice, human dignity and liberation.

Each year we produce two issues of our journal Socialist History, one or two historical pamphlets in our Occasional Publications series, and frequent members' Newsletters. We hold public lectures and seminars mainly in London. 'In addition, we hold special conferences, book launches and joint events with other friendly groups.

Join the Socialist History Society today!

Members receive all our serial publications for the year at no extra cost and regular mailings about our activities. Members can vote at our AGM and seek election to positions on the committee, and are encouraged to participate in other society activities.

Annual membership fees for 2018 (renewable every January):

Full UK £25.00
Concessionary UK £18.00
Europe full £30.00
Europe concessionary £24.00
Rest of world full £35.00
Rest of world concessionary £29.00

For details of institutional subscriptions, please e-mail the treasurer on francis@socialisthistorysociety.co.uk.

To join the society for 2018, please send your name and address plus a cheque/PO payable to Socialist History Society to: SHS, 50 Elmfield Road, Balham, London SW17 SAL. You can also pay online.

Visit our websites on www.socialisthistorysociety.co.uk
and www.socialist-history-journal.org.uk.

Some Recent Occasional Publications

28 Deborah Lavin	*Bradlaugh contra Marx. Radicalism versus Socialism in the First International*	£4.00
29 Willie Thompson	*Setting an Agenda, Thomson, Dobb Hill and the Communist Party Historians*	£3.00
30 Richard Hart	*Caribbean Workers' Struggles*	£6.00
31 Marilyn J Boxer and John S Partington (eds)	*Clara Zetkin: National and International Contexts*	£7.00
32 David Goodway	*The Real History of Chartism or Eight Fallacies about the Chartist Movement*	£3.00
33 Christian Høgsbjerg	*Mariner, Renegade & Castaway: Chris Braithwaite – Seamen's Organiser, Socialist and Militant Pan-Africanist*	£4.00
34 Duncan Bowie	*Our History. Roots of the British Socialist Movement*	£4.00
35 Frank Tanner	*British Socialism in the Early 1900s*	£6.00
36 Malcom Chase, Willie Thompson and David Parker	*Eric Hobsbawm: Socialist Historian*	£3.00
37 ed. David Morgan	*'Stop the First World War': Movements Opposed to the First World War in Britain, France and Germany*	£5.00
38 John Newsinger	*Sylvia Pankhurst, the easter Rising and the Woman's Dreadnought*	£3.00
39 Steve Cushion	*"Killing Communists in Havana" The Start of the Cold War in Latin America*	£4.00
40 Robert Turnbull	*Climbing Mount Sinai Noah Ablett 1883-1935*	£4.00
41 ed. David Morgan	*1917, The Russian Revolution, Reactions and Impact*	£6.00

Many of these titles are still available post free from:

SHS
50 Elmfield Road
Balham
London
SW17 8AL